The Good Ground of Central High

The Good Ground
of Central High

Little Rock Central High School
and Legendary Coach Wilson Matthews

An original nonfiction story about a high school football player and
the values he learned from his successful and sometimes difficult coach.

George M. Cate

BUTLER
CENTER

BOOKS

The Butler Center for Arkansas Studies
Central Arkansas Library System
100 Rock Street
Little Rock, Arkansas 72201

First Edition, 2008

ISBN (hardback) 978-1-935106-02-9
Hardback printing: 10 9 8 7 6 5 4 3 2 1

ISBN (paperback) 978-1-935106-03-6
Paperback printing: 10 9 8 7 6 5 4 3 2 1

Acquired for Butler Center Books by David Stricklin
Project manager: Ted Parkhurst
Project editor: Marcia Camp
Book design and cover design: H. K. Stewart
Cover photograph: The author in his LRCHS Tiger uniform, 1950.

Photographs used in this book are the property of the author or were secured for use in this book by the author.

Printed in the United States of America

This book is printed on archival-quality paper that meets requirements of the American National Standard for Information Sciences, Permanence of Paper, Printed Library Materials, ANSI Z39.48-1984.

To my brother Eddie Bradford

The ties that bind are many strings, and their names are fear and courage, want and sharing, pain and healing, folly and redemption, pride and humility, defeat and victory ... both for two Tigers from Seventh Street and a thousand Tigers from everywhere.

Eddie Bradford, number 77, in 1950

You've got it all underneath your feet.
There's room to grow—there's time to breathe,
and dreams stretch high under summer skies.
This is where I'm from—this is who I am -
down these roads I became a man,
and they're calling me where my roots run deep,
deep down—this is good ground.

From "Good Ground"
by John Michael Montgomery

Contents

Acknowledgements

The annual number of new book titles produced in the United States is in excess of 50,000. For many of these authors, having their book printed is a high honor, made even more so if the sales are respectable and/or the content is praised. Likewise, being introduced as "my son (or daughter) the author" is a special experience.

For the first-time author (which I am) there are many discoveries. Far and away the most important one is the need for constant encouragement and support. You need this even if the person you rely on is simply being diplomatic in order to spare your feelings, if they have to be diplomatic to spare your feelings.

The possibility that you will not finish the book or, if you do, that it may not be very good, are specters that constantly play with your mind. This is such a common phenomenon, other writers have written about it. Their advice is usually the same—ignore these feelings—keep going, and don't quit. This is good advice.

Truth be told, there are times when the writer is nothing more than a secretary taking dictation. Just who is doing the dictating is hard to say, but one thing is sure—they know what they're doing. When they are through (whoever "they" is), so are you. They wear you out, but when you peruse what you have written you know one thing—you typed it, but you didn't compose it. So, whoever you are, wherever you are, the first acknowledgment is to thank *you* for those special sections you inspired me to write that are sprinkled throughout this story. I knew the tales, but you knew how to relate them.

On this earth, thanks must be given to Darice Bailer, a most prolific and erudite writer. She is a renaissance writer with credits ranging from children's books to books about the National

Prologue

This is a book about a trip I made one time. If you play football, or if you are considering doing so, you will probably make a similar one. Most trips we make are pretty straightforward. You know your exact destination, departure date and time, directions, etc. In short, trips are not normally mystery stories. Then there are the trips we take where we aren't even aware we are doing so. Think about that for a minute. You are making a trip, and you don't realize it. This book is about such a trip.

The United States has over one million boys who play football in approximately 14,000 high schools. Football is the fastest growing sport in the nation and exceeds basketball, the Number Two sport, twice over. In California and Texas, the interest in the game is extremely intense; they rank Number One and Two respectively in participation. Ten states, including California and Texas, account for 50 percent of all football players.

Statistics show that participation levels have steadily risen in the past 10 years. Numerous books about football are being directed at this target audience. Most of them are how-to books, greatest-games-ever-played books, and how-I-played-the-game books.

This book is not intended to be mainly about football. It's written for you, the high school football player. The purpose is to use the game with which you are familiar as a means of exposing you to ideas whose value and importance are greater than football, or any sports.

Publishers have asked me what kind of book this is:

Is it a sports book? I don't think so.

A book for adults? Somewhat, perhaps, but probably only for older former players.

An inspirational book? I hope some readers find it to be so, but if it is, this may be incidental.

How about autobiographical? Yes, absolutely, but that's not all.

This is a history book for young adults. The autobiographical part is my personal history, but it's still history. Then there's important world history that extended its tentacles all the way to Little Rock, Arkansas, and our school. There's also the history of the school and its football program.

Speaking of the program, it is now in its second century of operation. In 2007, *Sports Illustrated* referred to Central High School as "one of the country's greatest football dynasties." The foundation for such a label includes two national high school championships, several All-American high school players, a group of NFL players, numerous state championships (most of them consecutive), and an outstanding won/lost record against the champion teams from Texas, Louisiana, Oklahoma, Tennessee, and Kentucky. There were also victories over teams from Mississippi, and Alabama. As you will learn, building dynasties requires special coaches and special players.

The obligation of the school, the community, the nation, and religious institutions is to prepare you, the future leaders, to deal effectively with the challenges that lie ahead. Playing the game of football is one way of having a dress rehearsal for the responsibilities you'll be expected to assume later. That's what this trip is really all about.

The book you are about to read is also a history lesson. Studying history is meaningless if we don't gain insights into how to deal with similar challenges that await us. In this simple autobiography, you'll see most of the gut-wrenching experiences one can encounter in a lifetime. The list includes physical pain, victory and defeat, death of friends, war, inequities, good and bad behavior, friendship, and personal sacrifice. Quite a lot in only three years, and quite a trip, wouldn't you agree?

Now here's some good news. No teacher is going to test you on this book! Even better news—throughout this wonderful land of America your fellow countrymen in thousands of high schools are also learning the same lessons you are learning, just by playing football.

Your simple act of playing the game will gain entry into one of the most splendid fraternities—the fraternity of football players. Whether you're a star or not, whether you play for a large or small school, high school, college, or pro, it doesn't matter. For the rest of your life, you'll belong to this fraternity because you satisfied the most important prerequisites—you paid your dues by playing as well as you could, and you made the sacrifices required. Enough said. You're in.

When the time comes to hang the cleats up for good, don't forget what you've learned. You know how to slam a shoulder into a blocking sled, and you can now do the same to prejudice in all its ugly manifestations. As you read this book, it may come as a surprise to you to learn the Tiger football program had a black man on staff who was quietly undermining racial prejudice in a modest way several years before the infamous integration crisis in 1957. He accomplished this through strength of character, and his story is recounted here fully, perhaps for the first time ever.

You'll learn how to place the team's best interest above your own, and you'll have plenty of opportunities to do this again in your role as a father and family man, as an employee and later as a boss, and as a citizen in your community.

Football teaches you how to keep going when your body and mind protest that you just can't—but you do. You do because you have pride, and pride is stubborn. You may need to do this again some day in military service, or it may mean staying up for hours tending to a sick child, but you will do it and do it well.

There'll be days when football knocks you on your tail, but you get up, recover, and stay in the game. You'll have to do this again most likely, and you will. You will know what it's like, and you'll know it's something that has to be done.

Most likely your coaches will teach you to play fairly and not to retaliate when your opponents break the rules. That's still a good rule to live by. Football will teach you to prepare your body, mind, and soul to play the game. That's easier said than done but you'll know how because you will have done it before.

You may be a little curious about the meaning of "Good Ground" in the book's title. This is a term used in different settings but most often in religious or military ones. For the time being, let's just say it refers to everything about Central High, and your school as well, that helps football players realize their potential as men and leaders. We'll revisit Good Ground again in the Epilogue. Hopefully, when we reach that point, you'll be better prepared to understand its meanings, especially as it pertains to you personally.

One final point, practically everything I learned came the hard way. Please remember, the reason we study history is to avoid having to repeat it. On behalf of older men who know what lies ahead for you and who want to support you in any way possible, take these few pages that follow as our sincerest offering to you. We wish you Godspeed.

George M. Cate
#66 Right Guard
1951 Little Rock Central High School Tigers

Introduction

Once every five or ten years I have this dream. The plot is always the same, namely that I'm a starting guard for the Little Rock Senior High School Tigers football team, that we are in the middle of a game in Tiger Stadium, and that my participation is crucial to the team's success. The dream always reveals that I'm ineligible to play because I've already graduated. But wait, there's no problem because a mistake was made, and I really am still eligible! I know it's okay for me to be in this game because the coach, Wilson Matthews, says he needs me, and it's crucial for me to play. Then I experience high exhilaration. Once this happens, the dream ends.

The truth is this: when I played for Coach Matthews, I was just a substitute. Insofar as eligibility is concerned, he probably would not have considered it a burning issue. Just why I was a sub and not a regular starting guard is the main story. As you'll see, it was largely my fault, although for years I felt otherwise. It took a long time, but eventually we worked things out, or, I should say, I worked things out.

During the time I played in 1949-1951, Wilson Matthews was a kid coaching kids. He was only in his twenties, and, chances are, upon more mature introspection in his later years, he might have done some things differently in his approach to handling young men. Maybe not. His record is so good he may have chosen not to change anything.

Even as a young coach, he managed to raise some eyebrows around town. His tirades on the field were often a subject of conversation, but note was also taken of his superb won/lost record. With regard to his record, his detractors dismissed it as the inevitable result of having a wealth of talent at his disposal. They conveniently overlooked the point that poor coaches are fully capable of misusing talent or making other mistakes. However, one is not likely to get away with the simplistic assertion that talent explains everything.

Speaking of records, his are pretty impressive. In 11 years as a head coach, he won 109, lost 17, and tied 3; won 10 state championships, and one national championship.*

Do the math, and you'll see there was one year when his team did not win a state championship. That would be the 1951 team. The one on which I was a sub. The '51 team had a 9-3 record, which for most schools would be a very good year. However, this rule did not apply to Little Rock Senior High School. Our standards were higher. By our self-imposed standards, 1951 was a terrible year, and this business of standards had a lot to do with why I wound up as a substitute.

With Coach Matthews, what you saw was only a portion of what you got. His knowledge of football was never in dispute, and he always seemed equal to, or ahead of, his time. He was also a no-nonsense disciplinarian, to the point that, when he occasionally loosened up, it was almost a special occasion.

Sometimes his temper eruptions took on a comical twist that made his players want to burst out laughing. When Coach was really exasperated he would throw his baseball hat into the air. A team manager was usually nearby to pick it up and hand it to him. The cap-throwing eventually became so frequent, and so predictable, team manager Charlie Rea became adept at catching it in mid-air. Each time he did this, players would turn away to hide their laughter. Eventually, Coach told Charlie to just let it fall on the ground.

*Tiger Pride, Brian Cox, Arkansas Business Ventures, 2005

But he had another side that was intensely private. Virtually no one knew, or even imagined, it existed. Quietly over the years he helped many of his players who had special needs and problems, and he didn't call the newspapers to let them know what he'd done. He was known to keep track of various former players and how they were doing in their jobs and personal lives. In a sense, having been a member of his team was often a lifetime entitlement to his interest and concern. When he died, his personal effects included a large number of thank-you letters he received over the years from former players. Often they were writing to thank him for having been so tough.

He also had a dimension that was virtually impossible to understand. His temper was legendary. There were times when he lost it, and the players involved were hard-pressed to understand or explain what they had done to cause his outbursts. Sometimes his displeasure crossed the line to becoming mean-spirited.

Consider this. Fifty years after he left Little Rock, there is a former players club called "Wilson's Tigers." Members of his old teams regularly meet for breakfast every day at a Little Rock restaurant. When his players meet from time to time, you can hear them use his favorite figures of speech. He often began a sentence with the phrase "I'll venture to say …"

I'll venture to say that Wilson Matthews can be better understood by conversing with his players, one at a time. This book is my time.

Wilson Matthews, head football coach, Little Rock Central High School Tigers

Chapter 1
Homecoming

"Welcome to Little Rock," the United Airlines flight attendant said shortly after the plane landed.

Welcome indeed, I thought to myself—it's hard to believe I'm really here. But like all of the out of state alumni, after a year of letters, emails, and phone calls from Ethel Roberts Curry, Tandy Allen, Crys Bell Waite, and several others (along with a push from my wife, Arlene) I was really here. I had run out of excuses not to attend the 50th reunion of Little Rock Senior High's Class of '52. The last reunion I attended was the 25th. Its venue was one evening event, and the theme of the meeting had been to pay tribute to the former football coach, Wilson Matthews.

The school that had become Little Rock Central High School scheduled a 50th reunion that was considerably more ambitious. The first get-together was a buffet dinner on Friday evening, a Saturday morning tour of the high school, and Saturday evening a sit-down dinner at the Little Rock Country Club. Sunday morning, a brief memorial service was offered in honor of our deceased classmates, followed by a brunch in the Arkansas Arts Center at MacArthur Park. This was a reunion guaranteed to keep you busy, not including a hospitality room at the Marriott Courtyard Hotel that appeared to be open round-the-clock.

Saturday morning was rainy. Perhaps for that reason, less than a hundred people showed for the class picture in front of the school. After the photographer was finished, Ethel Curry told everyone to wait because she wanted to introduce the current principal. He was a distinguished looking man who quickly engaged the attention of the group with his humor. He was also an African-American. The significance of this was not lost on those of us who had experienced the pain of seeing the school's image tarnished when the 1957 integration crisis erupted. The school was built in 1927, and was honored by the American Institute of Architects as the most beautiful school in America. Thirty years later, its physical beauty was completely overshadowed by the civil disturbances enveloping the school and the surrounding neighborhood.

The Principal noted that the school had been declared a National Historic Site in 1998, and accordingly received federal money for a much-needed renovation. He then invited us to enter the school and visit anywhere we wished. There were only two stops I wanted to make. The first was Room 236, my old homeroom for three years. The second stop was the school auditorium.

Room 236 looked exactly as it did 50 years ago. All it needed was our teacher, Mrs. Lee, to make it complete. The second stop was a disarming one. Standing in the back of the school auditorium, it was far larger than I recalled, and the stage itself was much wider than I remembered. I couldn't resist walking on it.

Facing the mass of vacant seats, I recalled my appearances on this stage. They included several school plays, plus an occasional appearance with my partner in comedy, Jim Wallace, to perform routines we had put together since our days at West Side Junior High School. But there had also been one other appearance on this stage, and it was one that was not pleasant. It had stayed with me until this day. More about this later.

My watch reminded me it was time to leave for a small lunchtime get-together with friends. As I left the building, I noticed the neighborhood surrounding the school. Fifty years ago the homes there were in good repair and presented an image of neatness and loving care, but that was 50 years ago. That day, many of them were ramshackle, hardly resembling their former glory. This section of town was not far from being a slum, if indeed it already was not.

My car's right turn into the nearby faculty parking lot would give me a chance to look down on the football practice field and Tiger Stadium situated below. (The official name is Quigley Stadium, but most people still prefer to refer to it as Tiger Stadium.) The luncheon could wait—this was an opportunity too good to pass up.

Maybe it wasn't such a good idea. The practice field seemed scraggly and untended. Weeds grew around the periphery. Perhaps, this was a temporary situation, considering that it was April, several months away from the next season.

Tiger Stadium was unmistakably down at the heels. The exterior walls were dirty sections with rust stains on some. The light tower standing just outside the entrance hadn't seen paint in a long time. It was a sad sight. Frankly, it was a picture of a facility that needed someone in charge who really cared. One time it had had such a person.

My mind's eye brushed aside the reality in front of me, and the field and the stadium were restored to their pristine condition of 1949. Now it was sunny and very hot. Dozens of young men stood in line to take their turn on the blocking sleds. Whistles blew and orders were barked. It was August 20, 1949, and this was the first day of football practice, courtesy of Head Coach Wilson Matthews and his two assistants, Howard Pearce and Ray Daugherty. The imaginary panoramic scene below had been waiting for a chance to come out.

Chapter 2
Getting Ready

In the spring of 1949, Coach Coy Adams posted a notice on the door of the West Side Junior High School gym. It announced there would be a meeting with Coach Wilson Matthews for everyone who planned to go out for football at Little Rock Senior High School next season. For the rising 10th grade boys, this was not a meeting to miss.

The purpose of the meeting of about 20 boys was orientation. Coach Matthews covered some of the basic procedural details. You would have to pass a physical examination by the team doctor, and you would need your parents' permission to go out for the team. Above all, he said, you must be in shape when you show up for the first day of practice.

Smoking was strictly forbidden. We were told to avoid carbonated drinks. "Bad for the wind." From the minute he said this, I didn't drink a Coke or any other carbonated drink until I was a college freshman. Tru-Ade, a popular non-carbonated soft drink, became my drink of choice. I wasn't about to let a Coca Cola ruin my chances of making the team.

This was the first opportunity I had to meet Coach Matthews, if you call sitting in a group as "meeting." His reputation preceded him and word-of-mouth basically portrayed him as a tyrant. When he spoke to us, however, I was impressed with his serious demeanor and how his style was more akin to man-to-man, not man-to-boys. Looking back, I see this was an important technique that underlaid his approach to coaching young men.

Coach Adams, my junior high coach, had played for the Tigers in 1931, and was a three-year letterman. During the two years I played for him, he made frequent references to the difficulty we would experience at the high school level, and he used this as motivation for us to learn the basics of football as well as possible. Coach rarely used profanity, and he seldom ever lost his temper unless something or somebody seriously provoked him. In short, there was virtually nothing in our experience with Coach Adams that prepared us for our encounter with Wilson Matthews. These two coaches were about as different as two men could be.

Sophomore Year

Chapter 3
Meet Mr. Johns

As the August 20th date for practice approached, my friends Dick Gladden, Ed Rutledge, and I decided the time had come to start getting in shape. (The fact we had already wasted two months seemed to have passed us by.) What better place to do this than at Tiger Stadium, and what better way to make a good impression on the coaching staff than to show up for workouts a few days in advance of the official start of practice? With this strategy in mind, we agreed to meet at the stadium around 10:00 one morning to get started.

Finding the stadium entrance conveniently open, we were about half way into the lobby when a voice from the shadows bellowed out "Hey, what do you guys want?" Startled, we turned to see a black man looking at us in a very disapproving manner. Gentlemen, meet Riley "Doc" Johns.

"We're here to work out," I stammered.

"Work out where?" he asked.

"Why, inside on the track."

"Y'all get out of here. You're not working out in this stadium, and let me tell you something else—don't be dragging your tails in here in the middle of the morning to work out. Be here at seven or eight, and use the practice field."

That barrage had the three of us stumbling over each other to leave. So much for our strategy.

We'd just had our formal introduction to Riley "Doc" Johns, Tiger team trainer, and also the person in charge of maintaining the stadium and its grounds. He and his family actually lived in an apartment in the stadium, so in a sense you could say that the football complex was his domain.

Riley "Doc" Johns, official trainer

Before our misbegotten appearance, we were vaguely aware of Riley Johns. We had heard about this black man who was treated like a white man by the coaches and players. We had also heard that occasionally he would coach in practice, and that he had been known to make observations to the coaches that proved to be helpful. His main job, however, was to tend to the bumps and bruises of the athletes for all school sports, and to manage the upkeep of the stadium and its practice field. (Construction of the stadium was completed in 1936, at a cost of $100,000, a fraction of what it would cost to build today.)

I know almost nothing about Riley Johns' background. According to Brian Cox in *Tiger Pride*, Riley "Doc" Johns originally came to Little Rock in 1928, to serve as the trainer for the Arkansas Travelers professional baseball team. Once here, he quickly migrated to the Tigers as their trainer.

What I can say from personal observation is that he was handsome, articulate, and mannerly. He was a gentleman, and I observed this on several occasions. When approached by a lady faculty member, he would doff his hat and make liberal use of "Yes ma'am" and "No ma'am." His tone of voice was friendly, and his body language was cordial. His contact with male teachers was businesslike and polite. His manners were a model for the young players who observed him in action.

What I also eventually learned is that Doc loved the players. He had a sense of humor, and he knew how to chide them, especially in groups, that was sure to bring out laughter and comebacks. If Doc chided you, you knew you were accepted.

Our first meeting with Doc boiled down to the fact that one mid-morning appearance at the stadium was not much of a commitment, and the idea of getting into proper shape a few days before practice started was ridiculous. On that particular day we neither understood the meaning of "commitment" nor "shape," but that was all about to change.

Chapter 4
The First Day

In 1949, Little Rock had three white junior high schools—East Side, West Side, and Pulaski Heights. (It also had only one public high school for whites and one high school for blacks.) Each junior high school had a football team and all three schools played each other during the regular season. We did not, however, have an opportunity to get to know opposing players off the field.

The first day of practice, there was the chaos of assembling together in the locker room, without benefit of introduction. There were several scuffles as well as snarls and thinly veiled attempts at intimidation. It would take a while before the suspicions and doubts about our new teammates would turn into acceptance and friendship. We didn't understand that aliens from other schools would become lifelong friends.

The coaching staff consisted of Wilson Matthews, head coach, Howard Pearce, line coach, and Ray Daugherty, junior varsity coach. The schedule for practice was similar to that of most high schools, colleges, and pro teams even today. Morning practice from 8:00-10:00 a.m., and afternoon practice from 3:00-5:00 p.m. The morning practice attire was shorts and tee shirts, cleats, and helmet. The afternoon practice was full uniform and pads. Morning practices were viewed as being much easier. Except for the first morning practice on the first day. For me it was nearly a disaster.

That morning was more mob scene than practice. There were wide-eyed young boys intermingled with older players whose bass voices conveyed an aura of aggression and superiority. To the new and younger players they were almost like adults.

After an opening round of calisthenics, which convinced a few of the young aspirants they should choose another sport, we were organized into groups—linemen in one area, backs and receivers in another. Membership in a group was self-determined. If you thought you were a fullback, you went with the backs. If you thought you were a tackle, you followed the linemen to their group. I was a center in junior high school, and planned to continue in this position.

Coach Matthews approached the lineman group and took a general survey by a show of hands as to which of us wanted to be guards, tackles, and centers. I held my hand up for center—almost no one else wanted to play center.

At this stage of events, it was not possible for him to know our names. Often we were identified by some physical characteristic. In my case, I was immediately named the "center-with-big-legs." As an ungainly adolescent, my body had not yet matured evenly. My thighs and legs were very muscular and disproportionate to the rest of me, but from the time I received this moniker, any call for the center-with-big-legs meant me. That call came soon.

Coach directed me, the center, to line up with two guards and two tackles. A blocking bag stood in front of each of us. The drill was this: Coach would call a play, and, on the snap count, each of us would perform the blocking assignment appropriate for that particular play. I panicked!

In the split second between the times the play was called and the snap count barked, I realized I didn't have a clue about my blocking assignment. First came the snap, and then came a barrage of epithets! Not knowing what my assignment was, I simply blocked the dummy in front of me. This was not correct, and I wasn't the only lineman to do it. Another play was called in quick order, with the same result.

Facing the blocking bag and not Coach Matthews, I heard a steady stream of reprimands. Out of the corner of my eye, while I was in a three-point position facing downfield, I saw Coach's foot heading in my direction. Fortunately, it stopped a yard or so before contact, so I was only hit with some sod.

That did it! We were all dismissed from the drill. In fact, the entire practice was adjourned, not altogether a bad development since my main objective for the moment was to get out of Coach's sight. The first morning of the first day was a disaster, and the day wasn't even over.

The time from 10:00 a.m. to 3:00 p.m. was frantic. The afternoon practice was almost certain to involve the same drill. Unless something changed, the same result was a certainty.

First a situation analysis: how do you find out what the plays are, and how do you know what to do for each one? (In junior high we never had a playbook.) To the best of my knowledge, there had been no advance notice about a playbook, or any other guidance. That didn't mean it hadn't happened, but I was out of the loop if it had.

Second, who can help me between now and three o'clock? My answer, and it was a good one, was to call my best friend—Eddie Bradford.

Eddie was a junior, had been on the varsity since the first day he ever reported for practice, and had been my close friend since 1939, when we met as little boys on a vacant lot between his house and my apartment house. We lived on Seventh Street directly across from the Arkansas State Capitol building. A year older than I, Eddie was often my protector when I was picked on by older larger boys. This time I really needed his help.

Fortunately, he was home. He was sympathetic, and he knew exactly what my problem was. In the short time available, he gave me a few tips that would enable me to get through that afternoon. He warned me that this was only stopgap—what I had to do was get a playbook and study it religiously.

When afternoon practice began, we didn't repeat morning drills. Instead, we were introduced to the blocking sleds. Both sleds were made of wood, and each had a name. The one I took turns on was called "Sunstroke." With a coach standing on the back of the sled, two players would slam into the padded frame and propel it forward. As the weather got hotter, we developed an undisguised hatred for Sunstroke. The coaches were never satisfied with our performance, and this intensified our animosity toward the sleds.

(Two years later, on a very hot day, Sunstroke showed signs of deteriorating. Realizing we now had it within our ability to destroy this beast, we attacked it with blocks of unusual ferocity, not unlike what a lion does to a hapless hyena. Before the practice was over, old Sunstroke was only a pile of broken boards. Hundreds of former Tigers would have cheered this feat.)

The next activity was what is sometimes known as the blocking pit. In this drill, two blocking dummies are separated about three feet apart. One defensive lineman faces an offensive lineman and one running back. The object is for the defensive lineman to fend off the block of the offensive lineman and then tackle the back, while not going outside the boundaries of the dummies.

The blocking pit is one of the most violent drills in football. Invariably someone will be hurt, usually in the face, with ample blood and gore forthcoming. For linemen, it is perhaps the single, most important determinant of talent for football. When you observe it, you sometimes wonder how anyone will get up when it's over. When you are a participant, you hope and pray you won't look bad and that you can make the tackle or protect the back. Above all, you want to look respectable, but we soon learned that very few performances were good enough—you were always expected to do better, and when you performed poorly, the coaches let you know about it.

Afternoon practice ended with a scrimmage, mostly involving the experienced players. I was glad to stay on the sidelines and observe. Today the center-with-big-legs had no interest in any more exposure. When practice was over, I went home, ate dinner, then straight to bed, so tired I went right to sleep.

Chapter 5
The Blooding

As the hot days of practice continued, old problems like playbook assignments were solved, and new ones took their place. The most challenging one was to demonstrate you had enough potential to make the team. That included the intangible of nerve.

Toward the end of the first week, Coach Howard Pearce presided over a late afternoon scrimmage, with particular emphasis on defense. I was made middle linebacker, and he stood almost right behind me as though his one and only interest was to evaluate me. I was skinny and weighed about 160 pounds. There wasn't too much to evaluate.

The first encounter with Pearce could be intimidating. Behind his back the players nicknamed him "Hippo" because his facial features sometimes took on the countenance of an angry hippopotamus. It was rumored he had once played for the Cleveland Browns professional football team. Whether he had or not, he certainly looked the part. He was stocky, muscular, and he had a direct, no-nonsense way of communicating with players. He wasted no time applying it to me.

The first few plays from scrimmage stopped at the line of scrimmage. Immobile, I stood and watched as though I were a spectator. Coach then inquired why I had not met the play on the line, or better, in the backfield. I said I didn't know I was supposed to do anything until the play reached me where I was standing. A tutorial just for me ensued. The object was to teach me that football was a contact sport and that, henceforth, he wanted to see me crash into the offense and tackle somebody.

After several more attempts, I succeeded in penetrating the offensive line and assisted in making a tackle. I acquired a small facial cut in the process and soon heard Coach hollering "that's more like it; keep it up!" He also smiled at the blood on my face, and his look told me that it was as good as a battle ribbon.

In olden times when men settled their differences by dueling with swords, their opponents would often receive facial cuts that would bleed and leave scars. Your manhood might be called into question if you had no scars, as this usually meant you had never engaged in combat. Whenever you were cut this was called "blooding," and it was usually considered a sign of honor and a rite of passage, even if you had lost.

That night I had a date with Ethel Griffin, and I made sure I had a Band-Aid over the tiny cut as if it were a ribbon. Many of the players had bruises and cuts. I hoped my small, insignificant wound meant that I would be taken seriously as a player.

This first one-on-one encounter with Coach Pearce provided as clear a signal as anyone could receive concerning what he meant when he said something. However, my receiver wasn't always turned on. For example, on one occasion he voiced concern that we were not very good at blocking punts. He told us to rush the punter and make every effort to spread our bodies so as to repel the ball. The ball might hit you in the chest or in the stomach, or even in the face (in those days there were no nose guards on the helmet). No matter, just make sure you blocked the punt with some part of your body.

He also told us to forget about getting hurt by a kicked ball. "You've got a helmet and shoulder pads and rib pads and hip pads and thigh pads, You're not going to get hurt, so I want to see you rush the punter, and I don't want to see anyone dodging the ball or trying to avoid getting hit." But on the first few attempts, dodging the ball is exactly what we did—we didn't block anything.

"Do that again and you're going to be sorry," he said.

Try as we might, our next effort wasn't much better. Then out of the blue came a bullet pass straight for the head of the guy who ducked.

"You can block the darn punt or get your bell rung. It's your choice."

I once saw a western movie that had a bar scene where a rattlesnake was coiled in a glass box. You could bet that if you put your hand on the glass, you'd flinch if the snake struck. No one was able to avoid flinching, and so it was with blocking punts. Your natural instinct was to avoid having the ball slam into you, but this was an instinct that could be overcome with practice. A bullet pass to the head could overcome a lot of instinct.

Chapter 6
How Do Ya Do?

There were three elementary schools that channeled their graduates to West Side Junior High School—Centennial, Kramer, and Peabody, which was my school. In 1946, the boys of the entering Seventh Grade Class began the process of getting to know each other, making friends, and finding out who was the best and worst in sports, fighting, and scholastics. Sorting this out took some time.

Now, as we entered the 10th grade in this gigantic high school, the assimilation process had to be repeated, but on a grand scale. The impressions you made off the field were carried forward to the on-field ones, and vice versa. If you were sized up as somebody that could be pushed around in the school, you could be pretty sure someone would try the same thing on the practice field.

One day early in the season, Malcolm was doing something a lot of guys did—escorting his girlfriend Dot to her next class. As they walked down the hall, four new 10th Grade players came up behind them and began to make insulting remarks about Dot. Malcolm asked them in a nice way to stop it, but they persisted until Dot reached her class. Then they scooted on down the hall, disappearing from sight.

Several other players observed this incident, and couldn't resist making some comment to Malcolm about it in the locker room. Meanwhile, Malcolm silently stewed about what had happened. The more he thought about it the angrier he became.

He finally developed a strategy to settle the score. Movie fans will recognize it as formula Clint Eastwood, with just one problem for Clint—Malcolm invented it 50 years earlier. One by one, he studied the routines of each of the four culprits—what classes they went to and when. Most importantly, he learned when each of them would be alone.

The first guy never knew what hit him. As he turned a corner to go to class, an arm and a fist fired out from an alcove, sending him sprawling..

"How do ya do?" Malcolm asked.

All this fellow could observe from the floor was Malcolm looking down, asking him if he had anything cute he wanted to say about Dot. No, he surely didn't. He did, however, have an urgent need to tell his three cohorts what had happened.

Mildly concerned, the second guy was traipsing down the hallway two days later, when he encountered Malcolm, who had been patiently waiting for him. He could not escape, however. Malcolm landed several punches, and that was that.

The remaining two culprits had figured out by now what was happening. As they walked down the halls, they were a comical sight, constantly looking in every direction to spot Malcolm, who did eventually ambush a third one of the group.

The fourth guy? Well he asked the school authorities for protection. All four of them became the laughing stock of the school, and none of them made the football team. They were viewed as a group of predatory jackals who got exactly what they deserved.

It was interesting to observe that some of the most respected players, who were without question able to handle a fight with no problem, usually went out of their way to avoid one if at all possible. This was not viewed as a weakness, but rather as a strength.

For example, one day a recent graduate joined us for a special workout. This fellow was the Arkansas Golden Gloves Heavyweight Boxing Champion and had been for several years.

His opponents seldom ever lasted longer than one or two rounds before he knocked them out.

As part of his workout, he approached a former teammate, Eddie Bradford, to engage in some type of boxing drill. Eddie looked at him and replied "Now you know this is the sort of thing where it's very easy for one thing to lead to another, and then the next thing you know we're in a fight. Isn't that right?" The Champ agreed, and that defused what might have been a volatile situation. (Several years later, Eddie became the Heavyweight Boxing Champion of the University of Arkansas.)

From his days in West Side Junior High School until he graduated from high school in 1952, Henry Moore was our leader. His reputation as a fighter was beyond reproach, yet he had very few fights. For years, however, he was challenged by a friend named Gene. Gene was a lightweight fighter, and he never lost a fight in intramural boxing. He also never lost a street fight, of which he had many. He would often chide Henry, "One of these days I'm gong to have to whip your tail." Henry would always change the subject with Gene, so they never did fight.

One day I said, "You know hoss, Gene has said for years he was going to whip your tail some day."

"I know" Henry laughed. "He just waited too long. By the time he got around to it I'd grown too big."

Chapter 7
Scrutiny

During the practice days of August, Coach Matthews would sometimes have an evening meeting inside the stadium in the east stand. Dressed only in our civilian clothes, such sessions were usually very pleasant. Before a meeting started the young men would often harmonize, providing an amateur chorus of sorts that was very pleasant to hear, especially because of its spontaneity and the nostalgia it evoked.

The purpose of the first such meeting I ever attended was one of Coach's annual sessions in which he would bring in a well-known high school football referee to brief us on new rules changes. This was one of many things Coach Matthews did to ensure that his players were well prepared.

At the end of his presentation the referee looked over the crowd and eventually fixed his glance on Eddie Bradford and Wayland Roberts, respectively the tackle and guard during the past season.

"Coach," he said, "I remember these two from a game last year, and I want you and them to know that I'll be watching them closely this year." No one, including Coach Matthews, had any idea what he meant.

"Last season when they were on defense, the line judge noticed that they would grab the offensive linemen by their jersey and then pull them forward and onto the ground. This created a giant hole that the middle linebacker ran through to tackle the ball carrier. Don't try that this year or we'll call a penalty."

The referee's anecdote caused the group to explode in laughter. Eddie and Wayland had a sheepish grin, and Coach Matthews even had a slight smile.

No discussion about scrutiny would be complete unless game films are included. Coach Matthews always had every varsity game filmed. It was a ritual, on the following Monday afternoon practice, to watch the film of Friday night's game, along with Coach's color commentary (and I do mean, "color").

The new players quickly learned that the camera was brutal. What it recorded was the truth. Neither what you thought happened, nor your best recollection. Not what your teammate told you he saw. There it was up on the screen—the absolute unvarnished, uncompromised truth, and sometimes the truth was ugly!

The first film session I ever sat in on was bad news for a player we'll call Swede. The film clip we were viewing showed the Tigers kicking off. Away from the play, with not a soul within 10 yards of him, Swede suddenly did a somersault. Stop the projector! Run that play again!

"Swede," hollered Coach Matthews, "what the heck were you doing?"

Before Swede could respond, line coach Howard Pearce shoved two folding chairs out of the way as part of his beeline streak to reach Swede. Now two coaches were interrogating him simultaneously.

What was the explanation? It was simple. Swede was caught up in his exuberance for the game, and, in his excitement, he flipped. Literally. If the game hadn't been filmed, no one would have ever noticed, but because of that one "scene" in the film, Swede always received special attention in every other film.

My own film debut occurred in 1951, against Hot Springs. Just before a kickoff, I vowed that I would set a new speed record for going down the field and tackling the kickoff return man. I did in fact run down the field at an exceptionally fast speed (for me), which clearly showed on the film. Then, surprise! Because I was running so fast, a defender merely stuck his arm out and tipped me off balance. The result? The ball carrier practically waved goodbye as I tumbled past him to the ground.

"Look at that, look at that, will you just look at that!" yelled Coach Matthews. "Who was that?" It was me of course. Then a voice from behind me in the dark room said, "Coach that's me." The voice belonged to my friend John Cochran.

"No John, no" I whispered to him, "it was me, not you." But John didn't believe me. He was absolutely convinced he was the one. Worse yet, so was Coach Matthews. Even when I publicly stated I thought it was me, both John and Coach insisted otherwise. Then, of course, John got the tongue-lashing that was rightfully mine. That didn't make me feel any better.

Sometimes life resembles a game film. Much of what you do is viewed and evaluated. If you perform well, it may help you. If it's bad, however, it can seem like a chain around your neck.

Chapter 8
Survival Skills

The most important lesson to learn in relating to Coach Matthews was to listen and not talk, and to learn from the mistakes others made that almost always brought a rebuke. For example, each year someone would ask Coach if we were going to practice on Labor Day. The answer was always "yes" although usually in a very sarcastic fashion. Whenever a new player asked him this question the older players gave each other the eye and hid their grins as they waited for the inevitable put-down the questioner was about to get.

Coach didn't like unsolicited advice from his players. Any suggestions, no matter how innocent or logical, were usually met with the standard reply of, "If you want to coach here go fill out an application with the School Board." Early on we learned to keep our ideas to ourselves. The suggestion box was always closed.

Then of course there was always some newcomer who would ask out loud when we would have a break. Until 1951, the answer was always "Never." In that year, however, the heat was so bad he actually gave us three breaks, while at the same time chastising us for it.

I learned that any dialogue with Coach Matthews had better leave no room for his interpretation that the player was disrespectful. One day Coach stood behind the varsity line, deciding what play to call. In this process he asked the left guard a question. Without changing his stance, the player merely turned his head slightly back toward Coach and rendered his answer of "yeah." This was unsatisfactory, and Coach proceeded to take three running steps toward him before kicking him solidly. As the player picked himself off the ground and faced his attacker, Coach hollered "Don't say 'yeah' to me. Next time put a handle on it." Little did I know at the time that three years later I would be involved in a similar incident with him.

As a general rule, Coach Matthews was unapproachable to his players. You spoke only when spoken to, and it was risky business to initiate a conversation with him because you never knew if it might be misinterpreted or otherwise cause trouble.

From time to time, I witnessed players, usually new and inexperienced, incur his wrath because of ill-considered questions or comments. We were all well advised to learn from their mistakes as part of our own survival. Coach was in charge, and the players weren't, and, as long as we remembered that, we would be okay.

It probably would have been appropriate to post a sign for the closet smokers on the team. The sign would read "Beware of trick questions." The coaching staff was death on smoking, and if you were caught in the act you were in big trouble. As a means of rooting out the violators, Coach Pearce would casually approach a player in the hall or cafeteria and ask this simple question, "Got a match?"

If the response to this question was to produce a matchbook, or even to attempt to locate it in his shirt pocket, this individual was in deep trouble. He would receive a stern lecture coming from behind clenched teeth. There might also be other warnings that poor performances in games will be attributable to smoking, so don't expect much sympathy if you're pulled out of the game.

There were smokers on the team, but they were few in number. Forty years later, some of those who never kicked the habit probably better understand what the point was.

Chapter 9
The Switch

Early in the 1949 season, something very unusual happened on a Monday practice day. Coach Matthews announced that he was installing a new system. More specifically, he was changing to a T Formation offense from the Single Wing offense used for many years.

The very notion of changing the system in one week is somewhat like junking a workable piece of machinery and replacing it with a new piece that was designed, built, and installed in five days. Most coaches would say it couldn't be done without disastrous results, but Wilson Matthews did exactly that and was successful.

The week he installed the new system was relatively easy. Younger players just watched the entire spectacle unfolding. Immediately it was evident that a T Formation type system was an explosive innovation. Running backs took handoffs and tore past the line of scrimmage, in sharp contrast to the slow manner that plays developed in the Single Wing.

The 1949 Tigers were state champions. Coach Matthews' interest in keeping abreast of innovations was a factor. Over 50 years later, I sometimes chuckle at the observations made by television football game color men regarding the complexity of modern professional football. Clearly it is complex, but some of the examples they cite are somewhat humorous to me. Here are some of the techniques Coach Matthews had taught us as early as 1949; audible at the line of scrimmage, trap plays, tackle eligible, screen pass, draw, zone defense, and establishing lanes for punt returns. In short, he was a student of the game, and he wanted his players to be so as well.

Chapter 10
The Big Game

The football squad consisted of two teams, the Varsity (A Team), and the B Team. The Varsity was mainly comprised of seniors, a few juniors, and possibly selected sophomores. The B Team was comprised of less experienced sophomore and junior players. The B Team played smaller schools as its schedule.

The B Team's first game was with Jacksonville High School located north of Little Rock. Jacksonville defeated us, and I didn't play a single down. On the trip home, several of us congregated in the back of the bus, and a certain amount of horseplay occurred. After all, the game itself had no significance, or so we thought. A voice suddenly cut through the din of jokes. It was Riley Johns, and he was not pleased. Was this game just a big joke he asked, his eyes clearly fixed on me.

"I don't know why you even came out for football," he hollered. He directed his anger at some of the others. Suddenly the entire bus became quiet, and we were left with our private thoughts about the point Riley was making, and whether he would pursue it further when we returned home. Mercifully he never spoke of it again, nor did he need to. We got the message.

Throughout the season the B Team played several other games, including the B Team of North Little Rock High School. The primary purpose was to give our squad game experience. However, as Coach Pearce frequently reminded us, we scrimmaged our Varsity every day, and it was a "lot better team than any team you're playing this year."

The season ended with the Varsity's annual Thanksgiving game with North Little Rock High School. As usual, the Tigers won handily, a game I watched from the stands.

With the season over, I came to the following conclusions: I'd learned a lot since last August; I didn't want to play center any longer because I couldn't make good long snaps to the punter; I should become a guard; and I was going to enjoy a break from football. With regard to the last conclusion, I couldn't have been more wrong.

Chapter 11
The Classroom

With football season over, my expectation that there would be time for other activities was soon in shambles. What I was about to learn was that, with Wilson Matthews, football season never ended.

I discovered that every member of the football squad was assigned to an eighth period physical education class. Only football players were in this class, and rather than free time, we were now required to attend a so-called PE class.

The first challenge was to find where the class was to be held. To understand this, you'd have to be familiar with Little Rock Senior High School. Comprised of at least four levels and extending one block long, there were nooks and crannies in this building that hundreds of students never even knew were there, even after attending school there for three years. Coach Matthews, however, managed to find a room for his players that was in an obscure classroom on the highest level of the school. I'd never seen it before, nor had most of the boys.

On the first day of class, he told us to memorize our assignments for our position. Although most of us believed we already knew these, we were to assume we were starting anew.

As an example, if the play was Drive Right 34, and the defense was a seven man line, the right guard's assignment was to block the defensive guard in front of him with his right shoulder in order to clear a path for the running back who would be coming right through the lane between center and right guard. In Wilson Matthews' playbook, there was a specific assignment for every position for every play, and was so indicated in the play diagram.

In a perfect world, every player was expected to carry out his assignment exactly as drawn.

Day after day Coach Matthews stood before the class and went over every detail of our assignments. He gave pop tests, which were graded, and he peppered the class with questions. As an instructor, he was excellent. He commanded attention at all times and sharply rebuked anyone who gave stupid answers or who showed they were not studying the various handouts he had provided. He was also very good at explaining his teaching points.

As the course progressed through the months of December and January, there came a time when we believed we knew our position assignments inside and out. Then one day he announced that we would now study what our assignments would be for every conceivable defensive formation and what the assignments would be for every other position, specifically including backs as well as linemen. Essentially, we were now required to learn everyone's responsibilities for every situation.

Players who knew the responsibilities of other players were more likely to have a big picture of game situations, and they would be able to understand what was going on and how to adjust. Also, players could more easily play a different position if necessary.

The productive use of the time available in the off-season was the mark of a great teacher as well as a splendid strategist. While his contemporaries at other schools were likely taking it easy, the Wilson Matthews machine never shut down.

Chapter 12
The Auto Mechanic's Room

When the classroom instruction was completed, our new home was the auto mechanic's shop, also in another remote and little known location. A cavernous hall supported by large concrete pillars two stories high awaited us. This was our workshop when the winter weather was especially bad. One might suppose that the concrete pillars would obstruct the workout area. That would be true only if one needed lots of space, however the pillars *were* the workout space.

Under the direction of Coach Pearce, the linemen were directed to block the pillar. Excuse me Coach, you don't mean a full speed block of the pillar, do you? After all, all we wore was tee shirts and shorts. Yes indeed, a full speed block is exactly what he meant.

Initially we still didn't believe him, and so our contacts were half speed at best. This provoked a loud reprimand from Coach Pearce, and a demand for total compliance. The first person to block full speed was Jimmy Miller. The predictable result was that Jimmy smashed his face and blood began trickling from his nose. The only sound he made was to call Coach's attention to the fact he was bleeding. Although Coach was no more than a yard away and had observed all that happened, he walked over to Jimmy as if to make a careful inspection. Then he wiped the blood from Jimmy's face with his hand and then wiped it all over Jimmy's tee shirt.

"Miller, this is only blood and you ain't hurt; do it again."

Jimmy Miller did do it again, as well as everyone else. And this is how we spent many wintry days, perfecting our stances and blocking techniques, and learning that blood and gore are not as bad as they look.

Chapter 13
More Full Speed

Eventually our eighth period PE class moved to the practice field. As long as the temperature was 25 degrees or higher and there was no sleet, snow, or heavy rain, we practiced. The uniform was tee shirt, shorts, and tennis shoes (sneakers hadn't been invented yet). Had we worn pads we would have been in violation of the state athletic association rules, but with our skimpy attire we were strictly legit.

Most of the time we ran the plays we had studied so earnestly in Coach Matthews' class. Occasionally he would want to run a new play, and when he did he actually asked if we would go full speed. The answer was always an enthusiastic YES. (No rule against going full speed as long as we weren't wearing football equipment and attire!)

So there we were, shivering in the winter weather, occasionally blocking and tackling as if it were a day in August, and propelling our preparation months ahead of other schools. Through the mere technicality of not wearing pads, we were saving valuable time for next fall.

Going full speed in shorts carried some risk, as I discovered one afternoon. In a full speed play where I was a defensive guard, I was hit with high and low blocks at the same time from the center and left guard. A muscle snapped in my knee so loudly even Coach Matthews heard it. My practice was over, and I was helped off the field.

Chapter 14
Dr. Johns

By the time I arrived home that night my knee was swollen and painful. My father suggested we see a doctor, but I brushed the suggestion off. However, after a fitful night with practically no rest, I was ready for some kind of help. When I arrived at school, Coach Matthews told me to go see Riley Johns.

In the training room of Tiger Stadium, Riley examined the knee with the careful touch of an experienced trainer, but he didn't say anything as he made his examination. This gave me the erroneous impression he didn't realize how much it hurt. To convey this idea, I moaned somewhat when he touched my knee again.

"All right now," he said, "it doesn't hurt that much." Of course, he was right. It didn't. As it turned out, the knee was not serious, and a week's rest per Doc's orders was sufficient to let me resume practice.

It takes a young player a while to understand an idea that most coaches embrace, and eventually the players do as well. There is a difference between hurt and injured. Stated as succinctly as possible, "Hurt (and pain) don't count." Injury, meaning something that damages your body, like a broken arm, is taken seriously. Pain—well forget it.

In my junior year I decided not to start in a game with the North Little Rock High School B Team because of a painful hamstring. I honestly didn't think I could play with it. As the game progressed, it was apparent that the player who replaced me was doing a great job. So great, in fact, I became concerned he might nudge me out permanently. So I asked Coach Daugherty if I could play. He approved, and I played the remaining three quarters and played well. Funny thing, though, when the game was over, my pain was gone.

This was the first experience I can ever recall whereby my mind demonstrated its power to prevail over the physical pain of the body, and it was unforgettable. This taught me two rules. The first is that you play with pain. The second is that nobody gives a darn about your aches and pains. If you want sympathy, go somewhere else. That's just the way it is in football, and that's the way it is in life.

This latest encounter with Riley Johns finally made me realize how much I respected him and how the several encounters with him, strained as they may have been, were helping me mature into a young man. He taught me the difference between hurt and injury.

During the season, late in the afternoon, Doc would watch practice. He would usually stand alone, wearing his usual attire of coveralls, black work shirt, and black baseball cap. A solitary figure, at times he seemed to be lost in his thoughts. Very often he was smoking a cigarette down to the last millimeter.

In 1950, we began to see less of Doc, and eventually we were told he was having some medical problems. One day Coach Matthews asked the players if they would fan out to the business community in Little Rock and solicit contributions to a medical fund for Doc. We carried with us an introduction sheet to show prospective donors so they would know our campaign was legitimate. The team canvassed all types of businesses, including gas stations, restaurants, retail shops, etc. I have no recollection of having been turned down by anyone, nor was there ever a need for a hard sell. Riley Johns was known throughout the city, and I don't believe anyone, including Doc, realized how well known he was.

Subsequently the entire school met in the auditorium to present the contributions to Doc. In accepting them, he attempted to thank the students for their assistance. Sadly, we could barely understand his remarks. Doc had cancer of the throat, and by then he had largely lost his ability to speak. Nevertheless, the audience knew what he meant, and he was given a tremendous reception. We would have him with us only a little longer.

Junior Year

Chapter 15
Call To Arms

The end of the school year in May, 1950, marked the time when high school boys, and particularly the athletes, sought employment for the summer. The work was almost always hard manual labor of some type, usually in construction. I was lucky enough to get a job with the Arkansas Highway Department in their factory in North Little Rock where road signs were manufactured. The salary was 50 cents an hour, and I was glad to have it.

One morning when my father was driving me to work, the car radio announced the stirring of hostilities in Korea. Looking straight ahead, almost as if he were talking to himself, he said, "I hope this damn country isn't going to get into another war."

My father, Horace Ivan Cate, was a veteran of World War II, during which he served as a medical technician with a mobile army surgical hospital (MASH). Through France and Germany, he had seen the price of war first-hand. His final stop was in Dachau concentration camp near Munich, Germany. The horror of this camp and the experience of treating the survivors so traumatized him that he experienced nightmares for several years after returning home. Now, less than five years after the end of World War II, the nation appeared to be on the threshold of entering a new war of unknown proportions.

The following Sunday found me, as usual, in the balcony of Immanuel Baptist Church. Reverend W. O. Vaught, Jr., approached the pulpit and scanned the congregation, left and right, up and down. His sermons were always masterpieces of public speaking. In the heat of a delivery he would sometimes become so intense he would rock on his feet, up and down, back and forth. Mostly bald, during some sermons his head would glisten with perspiration. In impassioned deliveries, deacons would often call out "Amen" as their concurrence with whatever point he was making. (Many years later, Governor Bill Clinton attended this church. When Rev. Vaught was on his deathbed, the governor took Rev. Billy Graham to meet him.)

On this hot Sunday in 1950, Reverend Vaught was uncommonly solemn.

"Friends," he began, "this talk of war in Korea is something we must pray to God does not happen. I am asking each and every one of you to fall on your knees, and let us beg God that this war does not come to pass."

The entire congregation slipped down from their pews and fell on their knees as best they could. (This church did not have the pull-down kneelers found in some Christian churches, so the congregants were literally placing their knees and legs on the floor. The space between pews was likewise limited and not designed to allow one to slip down to the floor.) Physical comfort, however, was not important at that moment.

What followed was an impassioned prayer by Rev. Vaught begging God to spare America from a war in Korea. His trademark prayers were usually so long they were sermons disguised as prayers, and this was no exception. When the service was over, the congregation slowly and quietly left the church, blinking at the bright Arkansas sun, hoping their prayers would be answered, but it was not to be.

On June 25, 1950, the nation's worst fears were confirmed. American troops stationed in Japan were rushed to Korea to blunt the invasion of South Korea from the north. One infantry officer who was there told me several years later the first contingent to arrive from Japan was ill-trained, ill-prepared, and ill-equipped. "They expected us to stop a tank with an M-1 rifle."

As the summer of 1950 progressed, the war in Korea went from bad to worse. Accordingly, National Guard units were activated throughout the country. The activation covered units in Arkansas, as well as a Marine reserve unit in Little Rock.

The Little Rock Marine unit's roster included Bobby Bradford and his younger brother Eddie, who was age 16, to be precise—too young to be legally in any military branch. In early fall, after the school year had resumed, the Marine unit was activated and was preparing to leave town for points in the Pacific. On their roster was a 16-year-old machine gunner named Eddie Bradford.

On a regular basis Coach Matthews would meet with his players in a section of the school auditorium. At one such meeting he startled me by asking me this question, "I understand that your father has political influence. Is that right?"

I quickly determined he was referring to the fact that my father was the chief administrative aide to Arkansas' new Governor, Sidney McMath. Governor McMath was recently swept into office on a veterans' reform ticket. A highly decorated veteran of the Pacific, he was well known throughout the Corps, and he retained his status in the Marine Reserve. My father was one of McMath's campaign managers. When the election was over, he joined the governor's staff.

My response to Coach's question was that my father might be able to help. Coach then informed me that his starting tackle, Eddie Bradford, would soon be leaving town with the Marines, and he was too young to be in this situation. (Coach Matthews himself had served in the Marines in World War II.) I said I would ask my father if he could help.

That night at dinner I repeated the conversation to my father, and he was immediately interested in helping if he could. Of all my friends he especially liked Eddie.

"The Marines don't need a 16-year-old machine gunner."

The next day he shared the problem with the governor, who immediately went to work. I was told that one call from him to the Pentagon was sufficient to obtain a discharge for Private Eddie Bradford. My father called Coach Matthews with the good news. I don't recall Coach ever speaking with me again about this matter. How close did Eddie come to going to Korea? Here's how Eddie tells the story.

"We were assembled at the depot waiting for our train. Just as we were about to board, a Marine officer called us to attention. He then called out my name and two other people. 'Bradford, you all fall out and get on the truck. You're not going.' "

How's that for a close shave? Ironically, Eddie did not know how his discharge came about until he read a draft of this chapter. No one, including Coach Matthews, ever told him.

Had he been old enough to go with his unit to Korea, Eddie would surely have seen combat, as did his brother Bobby. Bobby earned the Bronze Star for valor, which surprised no one who knew him. As an interesting footnote, after graduating from the University of Arkansas with both a B.S. and M.A. degree, Eddie became a career army officer, whose service included a tour in Vietnam and Korea.

One day later that fall, word spread among the team that a former player who was very much liked by Coach Matthews had been killed in a car accident. His name was Charles "Chuck" Gildehaus, Class of '49. Practice that afternoon was subdued, and Coach was obviously affected, although nothing was said. There were other casualties among players from years back (as well as from the regular student body) who served their country in Korea. Of those who came back, some were badly wounded, including loss of limb.

The Duke of Wellington stated that, "The Battle of Waterloo was won on the playing fields of Eaton." This famous reference to the English defeat of Napoleon in 1815, is a relevant and eloquent commentary on how in their formative years young men are groomed for their future (but unknown) responsibilities. This process takes place on hundreds of athletic fields throughout America, and, in 1950, Coach Matthews' players were receiving perhaps their first introduction to this reality. In addition to the ongoing Korean War, in eight short years they would know about Lebanon, and in 15 years they would be familiar with Vietnam. Still later they would become familiar with Grenada and Panama and Kuwait and Afghanistan and Iraq and ... and ... and.

Chapter 16
The Payoff

I viewed August 20, 1949, with great apprehension, as well I should have. On that date I was not in good physical condition, didn't know my plays and assignments, had no idea how to relate to Coach Matthews and the assistant coaches, and knew only a few of the players. All of these factors were handicaps that had to be addressed. And they were.

George M. Cate, right guard

The 1950 coaching staff (left to right): Ray Daugherty, assistant coach; Wilson Matthews, head coach; and Steed White, assistant coach.

One year later, I could hardly wait for August 20, 1950. If there was one word that described George Cate, it was *focused*. My entire existence became football. No time for girls, and not even time for family (who had conveniently decided to go on vacation and leave our house and family car available just for me). Perfect!

The first 10 days of practice confirmed with absolute finality the gospel preached to us during the previous 12 months. The starting lineup for the B Team took shape very quickly as the players learned the consequences of preparing, or not having prepared, for this day.

Not in shape and physically exhausted? Step aside!

Don't know your plays? Step aside!

Still don't know how to line up in a good three-point stance? Step aside!

Can't block or tackle well? Step aside!

Haven't learned how to pass-block? Step aside!

Young men with the physical and mental gifts to play football *didn't* because they had failed to make the necessary commitment. Each day some would turn in their equipment and leave because they had dug themselves into too big a hole. There wasn't time to catch up. Still others resigned themselves to a season of very little playing time.

All those days last winter in the classroom with Coach Matthews, the hours in the auto mechanics room where Coach Pearce fine-tuned our blocking stance and other techniques, and those wintry days in shorts outside where we ran plays over and over until we could do them in our sleep. There was a reason for all this, and the day of reckoning was August 20, 1950. My reward was to be selected as the starting right guard for the B Team.

My rapport with Coach Pearce was also definitely on the rise. On several occasions he would compliment me on something I did in practice. This emboldened me to the point that I thought I could make small talk with him. After I made yet another play he liked, I asked him if he had any chewing gum to spare. The instant the request left my lips I knew I had overreached. Looking at me with a sarcastic expression, he commented, "The coaching staff doesn't normally carry gum for the players."

What a stupid question I had asked, and what a devastating answer I got, and deserved. I never would have asked Coach Matthews for gum, so why did I try that with Coach Pearce? The lesson I had just been taught was to stick to business, don't waste your leaders' time, and quit trying to carry on a miniature public relations campaign.

Four years later on a fall afternoon I walked into my house and was startled to see Coach Pearce in my living room. He and my father were watching a pro football game on our new television set.

In those days in Little Rock, television sets were still a novelty, and only recently did stations start operating here. Prior to that time, the closest station was in Memphis, and at best the black-and-white picture was a ghostly image with raspy sound. In any event, my father and Coach Pearce had somehow developed a business relationship that was solidified by their mutual interest in football.

I was invited to sit with them and watch the game. On one play there was a terrific collision between two players. Coach Pearce looked over at me and smiled.

"Now that's the way to do it, isn't it George?"

I thought to myself, I must be having a dream, sitting here in my house with Coach Pearce, watching television, and more or less conversing as equals. (I didn't ask him for gum.)

Chapter 17
The Coaching Clinic

One day during our August practice, Coach Matthews made an announcement we could hardly believe. Coach Bud Wilkinson of the University of Oklahoma was leading a coaching clinic to be held in Little Rock on the campus of the Arkansas School for the Deaf, and we would be allowed to attend if we wished.

Legendary coach Bud Wilkinson of Oklahoma was one of Coach Matthews' greatest admirers, and vice-versa.

If we wished? Was he kidding? Count me in, Coach!

On the day of the clinic there were surprisingly few of our teammates present. We entered the auditorium and quietly took a seat in the very back. A man we didn't know was lecturing the audience that probably consisted of about a hundred coaches.

Most of them appeared to be young and in the same age group as Coach Matthews. They took copious notes and there was an interesting question and answer session taking place. Above all, it was impressive to see how serious these young coaches were.

In the afternoon, the clinic moved outside, led by

The three Tiger linemen who impressed Coach Wilkinson (left to right): Eddie Bradford, tackle; Wayland Roberts, Jr., guard; and James Cauthron, center.

Coach Wilkinson. He was impressive. Tall with fair skin and gray hair, he had a very congenial personality and a wry sense of humor. While making his remarks, the attending coaches gathered around him in a semicircle. Then he turned to Coach Matthews.

"Now, Coach, if you can lend me some of your players I want to demonstrate the proper way for an offensive line to charge forward at the snap of the ball."

Immediately, three players appeared—Jim Cauthron, center; Wayland Roberts, guard; and Eddie Bradford, tackle. What Coach Wilkinson wanted them to do was charge straight off the line at the snap count of two, which he would call. He must, however, have thought that they might not do this drill very well. Gentleman as he was, he prepared his audience in advance.

"Now they're just going to illustrate basically how this is done, but keep in mind that it takes time to get this technique down pat."

The three Tigers proceeded to assume an offensive stance. Directly in front of them were three other players holding a blocking dummy. When Coach Wilkinson called the snap count, an explosion occurred. As if part of one machine, Jim, Wayland, and Eddie lunged forward in perfect unison and crashed into the dummies. The sound that resulted must surely have been heard yards away. The instant it happened there was an audible gasp from the assembled coaches.

With the sense of timing of a great comedian, Coach Wilkinson looked at the crowd, took off his hat, and smiled.

"I've never seen that done better than how they just did it, and that includes my team." Wilkinson's team won the National Championship in 1950.

At day's end, we began to understand that coaching was a profession and that we were lucky enough to be part of a program that was led by the very best.

Chapter 18
Farewell To Doc

On a bright fall afternoon, Coach Matthews told the team that Riley "Doc" Johns had passed away. No one was surprised, but it was still a shock.

For many of us, this was the first time in our lives that someone we knew and liked had died. Understanding death was not yet one of life's experiences. Doc's passing seemed so incongruous. After all, most other things in our young lives were going well, so why was this happening?

The next day the school announced something truly startling. Doc's funeral would be held in Tiger Stadium. While the reaction of the players was totally positive, there was nevertheless a sense of amazement that anyone would have their funeral in the stadium, notwithstanding that in Doc's case nothing could have been more appropriate.

After all, Doc had been with the team for over 20 years. The stadium didn't exist when the school first employed him. Only later, as a government public works project, did Tiger Stadium come into being. Doc must have seen the stadium rise from the ground until the day it was completed. Then, after that happened, he lived in an apartment in the stadium until he died. Now, in a few hours, he would leave the stadium and the team that had inextricably become his entire life.

The funeral was held early in the afternoon. School was dismissed to allow all students who wished to attend. Most of the 1,500 chose to walk from the school to the stadium for the services. It was a silent procession, but just as I entered the stadium lobby, a girl walking in front of me was talking to her

Riley Johns' funeral, Tiger Stadium, 1951. The pallbearers were Tiger football players, including Wayland Roberts, Jr., Bob Duncan, Larry Jones, Jim Cauthron, Eddie Bradford, James Sewell, Drew Clements, and Carl Slaughter.

friend and then suddenly laughed out loud. The instant she did so she realized that she had done something inappropriate, although she meant no disrespect. Nevertheless, several people in her immediate vicinity reprimanded her, and she appeared much chastened as she entered the stadium. The students who were displeased with her were not athletes, and this indicated the widespread respect Doc had.

The services were held on the east side of the stadium. An African-American minister preached a rousing service that, from beginning to end, was a tribute to Doc.

"Riley Johns has scored an eternal touchdown."

Doc's pallbearers were Tiger football players, stricken with grief. Throughout the stadium audience, individual athletes could be observed weeping silently on this sad day. Then the time came to go to the federal cemetery several miles away on Roosevelt Road. The procession of cars was so long that, by the time my friends and I arrived, the graveside services were already over.

As we paused at Doc's grave, we belatedly realized that he was buried here because he had served his country in the U.S. Army in World War I.

Years later, the fact emerged that Doc was buried in the general vicinity of Alex Haley's

Funeral Rites
To The Sacred Memory
Of The Late

Mr. Riley Johns
Held At The
LITTLE ROCK HIGH SCHOOL STADIUM
Fourteenth and Jones Streets
TUESDAY, OCTOBER 24, 1950—2:00 P. M.
LITTLE ROCK, ARKANSAS

Doc Johns wearing his rarely seen fedora

father. Haley's famous book *Roots* was a smash hit on television in the sixties, as it dramatized Haley's search for his family's history from Africa to the United States.

The day Doc was buried was, and continues to be, irony piled on top of irony. The school honored him for his service and demonstrated its heartfelt respect by holding his funeral in the stadium. Yet, had Doc been simply an ordinary citizen of Little Rock, he would have had to sit in a segregated section if he came to see a game.

If Doc had had school age children, they would not have been admitted to the high school where their father worked. If Doc had not lived in an apartment in the stadium, he would not have been allowed to rent or own a home in the vicinity of the stadium because the area was segregated for whites only.

Sadly, the medical care Doc received was likely substandard. When players visited him in his last days, they found him essentially alone in the basement area of a white hospital. The facility was poorly lighted, and neither doctors nor nurses were in evidence. This was quite a contradiction for a man who would be honored with a Tiger Stadium funeral. Although he had cared for hundreds of high school athletes for over two decades, the healthcare system and the institution of segregation denied him even the most basic medical attention.

Harry Ashmore, Executive Editor of the *Arkansas Gazette* during the 1957 integration crisis at Central High, and who won a Pulitzer Prize for his editorials, once observed that in the North whites don't care how far above them blacks go as long as they aren't too close, whereas in the South whites don't care how close blacks are as long as they aren't above them.

Riley Johns was a phenomenon. He received respect from his white contemporaries and student athletes, but he did not demand it. The respect flowed naturally and was given freely. Never was the word "nigger" directed at him, but, if it ever had been, I'm confident that Doc's white kids would have straightened the miscreant out quickly and effectively, in the event Coach Matthews hadn't already done so. Doc could be over us, as he was, and he could be close to us, as he was, simply because he was a great human being.

Perhaps this is as good a place as any to talk about crying. Yes, crying. Football players cry. When they do, it is almost always out of some deep frustration they are experiencing. When a player reaches the point where he is overcome with emotion, his first instinct is to hide it and to seek out a private place to regain control of himself, but often the nature of his frustration is so powerful, and untimely, it picks its own time and place to occur. For many Tiger football players, perhaps even most of them, Doc was nearby, and he knew what to do and to say.

Their individual stories had common threads. Doc would listen, and he would console, and he would place his arm around their back. He would get to the bottom of what the problem was, and occasionally he would work behind the scenes to help a coach understand how something he had said to a player was hurtful and not constructive. If the walls of Tiger Stadium could talk, they would speak of scores of cases where this wise and understanding black man became a father figure for the moment, and when he was through speaking, but mainly just listening, the young man's world seemed better and more manageable.

Some of the huskiest, most ferocious, and talented football players received this compassionate attention from Doc. In most cases what happened was as private as a confessional. But the walls know, and the players know, and Doc knew that football players do cry, and when they do, which is admittedly rare, it helps if there is someone like Doc nearby. If the Little Rock Central High football program is a dynasty, then surely Riley "Doc" Johns, was a part of the foundation.

In the summer of 1951, I found myself, as usual, working on a construction job building a road in North Little Rock. I was the only white person on the project, other than the foreman. The other workers were young black men about my age who attended the black high school in Little Rock. Over time, as we got to know each other, I learned of their intense interest in Riley Johns' funeral. They had all heard stories about it in the black community, but were they really true? Were there really hundreds of white people there? Were the services respectful? Was the funeral really in the stadium?

I attempted to field their questions as best I could, while silently being amazed at their interest and curiosity. I knew Riley "Doc" Johns, and they didn't, because they couldn't attend Little Rock Senior High School. Now how's that for irony? And there's more.

About the time Doc passed away, there was a major construction project underway. It was a new campus field house that would accommodate the needs of the Tiger basketball team as well as those of the physical education classes. The editor of the school newspaper, Jerry Dhonau, had worked for a while as a team manager and knew Doc well. He wrote a column for the newspaper stating that the new field house should be named after Doc.

The newspaper's faculty advisor implied that other members of the school administration were very uncomfortable with this proposal (which Jerry could never confirm) and refused to grant permission for him to print his opinion. Jerry responded by resigning as Editor of the paper. He went on to major in History and English in college. After college he joined the staff of the *Arkansas Gazette*. As fate would have it, he was assigned to cover the integration of Central High. The paper won a Pulitzer Prize for its coverage of this story.

Shortly after Doc passed away, a special concert was scheduled featuring an area college choir. The college was a black institution and there was some apprehension that someone in the audience might make a disturbance of a racial nature.

The event began when the choir members walked on stage from the wings of the auditorium. Strangely, after they were positioned on stage, they did not sing or make any movement. Silence prevailed, and it was awkward. Then a small black coed limped on stage and took her place at the end of the front row of the choir. She was crippled, and she required the use of a small primitive crutch to walk. While she walked there was no sound in the auditorium. When she reached her designated spot, she turned and faced the audience, and the auditorium erupted in applause. The choir in turn began its performance, which was well received and during which only respect was shown by the audience. There simply were no incidents.

The culture of segregation was probably as entrenched in Arkansas as in any other southern state. Yet the tribute paid to Doc and the reception accorded the choir seemed to suggest a transition was slowly working towards an era of better relations. This reasoning is one explanation why the 1957 integration crisis was somewhat startling. Some citizens viewed Little Rock as an improbable location for what happened.

How lasting was the public's sentiment about Doc? We must fast-forward to 1987, to answer this question. The leading sports writer in Arkansas was Orville Henry of the *Arkansas Gazette*. He received a letter from a fan urging him to support the nomination of Riley "Doc "Johns to the Arkansas Sports Hall of Fame. His letter read as follows:

"I have no quarrel with the names you listed for the Arkansas Sports Hall of Fame checklist. However, there is one name which I think was left off for too long. That name—Riley Johns. Riley probably was the most popular person in Arkansas sports and athletics from the 1920s until his death in early 1950. He was much more than a groundskeeper and trainer. He was counselor, coach, father image, and arbitrator for thousands of "his boys" during those years. His treatment of injuries was not limited to members of the LRHS Tigers and the Travelers. If a North Little Rock Wildcat or a Pine Bluff Zebra or any other player needed help for an injury, Riley would cross the field to do whatever he could to help. I'm sure that you remember Riley and that you agree that he deserves to be in the Hall of Fame. Wilfred Thorpe. Little Rock." (*Arkansas Gazette*, August 12, 1987).

In 1988, 38 years after his death, the Arkansas Sports Hall of Fame honored Doc with its prestigious Meritorious Service Plaque, which was subsequently accepted by Little Rock Central High School because he had no surviving family.

An article in the *Arkansas Gazette* described Doc in more detail:

"It was tough on Riley sometimes when we went out of town," Wilson Matthews, speaking as the former football coach of the Little Rock High School Tigers, said recently. "He always sat on our bench well, hell, he was our trainer and, in a couple of towns, the crowds got on him pretty bad. There was a bad scene or two at hotels. I won't say it didn't bother him, but he could handle it. He could handle anything.

"Officially, Johns was the groundskeeper of Tiger Stadium (now Quigley Stadium), and the trainer, and equipment custodian of all sports. Unofficially, he was more like one of the coaches."

"He was a coach, at least in basketball," insists Buddy Coleman, a Tiger athlete of the mid-1940s who played for three state tournament winners. "Not in any formal sense—he didn't help conduct practice or talk during the timeouts—but he kept the team together, kept us all thinking in the right way,"

Matthews recalled "I guess the last game Riley knew anything about was when we played Tupelo early in the '50 season. He couldn't get out anymore, but he could see part of the scoreboard from his window. He said, 'Coach, I need to see some points up there next to "Tigers."' I couldn't promise him anything except we'd try, because Tupelo was pretty good, but it gave me something to talk about to the team. We got Riley enough points to win." (*Arkansas Gazette*, February 4, 1988)

So now we know, over 50 years later, that this beloved and respected and tolerant man spent the last hours of his life watching a portion of the stadium score board to see how his boys

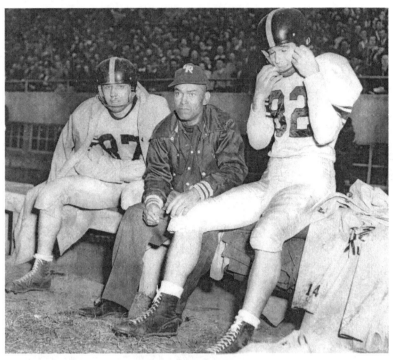

Chuck Devaney (#87), Riley Johns, and John Walker (#82) during a game

were doing on a Friday night. He could no longer talk, yet he was eloquent. His sense of sportsmanship, his volunteer work in the community, caring even for Tiger opponents, and the professionalism that characterized his work make him deserving of a higher title than trainer or groundskeeper. Distinguished Public Servant somehow seems more appropriate. Educator would likewise not be too extreme. There is perhaps one other thought to be gleaned from the Riley Johns story: Giants among men are sometimes found among the humble and in the most unexpected places.

Chapter 19
Thursday Night Football

The B Team for most boys was supposed to be the stepping-stone to the A Team (varsity). Although there were talented players who went straight to the Varsity in their sophomore year, for most of us the process was considerably slower. B Team was the way to show you were capable of being on the A Team by the time you were a senior.

The B Team played every Thursday, mostly at night but occasionally in the afternoon. The teams we played were in the conferences that were somewhat lower, because of school size, than the Big Six Conference our Varsity played in.

Most of our games were on the road, and we soon learned that they were akin to Custer going into the Little Big Horn. If your team could beat Little Rock's B Team, your season was a success. In candor, the Tigers had run up the score on teams in the past, and some little towns had long memories. According to *Tiger Pride*, Little Rock beat Russellville 174-0 in 1919, Paragould 90-0 in 1919, and El Dorado 70-0 in 1920, to list but a few.

Our first game in 1950 was with a little town called Bald Knob. Early in the game they fumbled the ball, and my friend Charlie Reed picked it up. "I got it," he hollered, "Let's go!"

Although it was entirely unnecessary, six of us escorted him down the field to score a touchdown. That one play set the tone for the whole game, which we won by a large margin. We were so high we hardly needed a bus to bring us home.

Friday morning my first class was study hall. Coach Matthews was in charge, but he had appointed me as his student assistant. He would be there briefly when the period started, but usually only long enough to get the game report from me. Usually his first question was "How did you all do last night? Did you run into a buzz saw?" Fortunately the answer was usually a favorable one, but sometimes it wasn't.

As a general rule, after only the first few plays you have a good indication of how long a night it is going to be. You always want to deliver your best possible blocks from the very beginning to let your opponent know you're going to be trouble. Once that message is delivered, things usually go well from that point on.

We won our first few games, which in turn gave us the idea we were invincible. While confidence was admirable, and probably even essential, there was a fine line between confident and egotistical. We crossed that line one night in a little town called Rison, population 1,400. Rison's coach was Sam Cook, and he was well known for his coaching prowess and expertise. He probably was qualified to be head coach at a much larger school, possibly even our school.

Each week in practice Coach Daugherty and Coach Pearce would rage at our mistakes. The standard line was "Just wait till you play some of these old small-town country boys that never get their name in the paper. You're not going to know what hit you." Rison must have been what they had in mind.

On our first offensive series, I slammed a block into the Rison defensive guard in front of me, and he didn't budge an inch. Succeeding plays produced about the same result. Whether on offense or defense (in those days you played both), the Rison players showed they were well coached and executed their assignments extremely well. Early on it was apparent that this was a team that wasn't going to roll over for Little Rock. I did manage to recover a fumble, but I only gained three yards before two guys tackled me. Rison won the game, and we couldn't get out of town quick enough. We had received what our coaches often referred to as a "country whipping."

The next morning as I trudged into first period study hall, Coach Matthews looked up from his morning paper, took one look at me, and cracked, "Ran into a buzz saw, huh?"

Perhaps the true buzz saw was the following week in a little town that shall remain anonymous. In our first practice for this game Coach Daugherty introduced us to someone who was going to help us prepare.

This individual was a referee, and he had officiated the game our upcoming opponent had played the previous week. Mr. X cautioned us that our opponent was unbeaten and that they had a most unusual strategy. When on offense this team used a formation that spread their players the entire width of the field. This tactic was highly confusing to the defense. Never having seen such an unconventional formation before, the defense was immediately in disarray, not knowing how to adjust. While the defense was trying to decide what to do, the offense was gaining big yards. Coach Daugherty spent a lot of time developing an adjustment and rehearsing it.

When the game started this team did not show the spread during the first quarter. In the second quarter, however, they did. The crowd started cheering, anticipating that Little Rock would soon be demolished. To the contrary, however, we simply performed as we had rehearsed, which was basically to spread out the width of the field with them, essentially on a man-to-man basis. This proved highly effective, and our opponent did not score. It also served to make the crowd angry.

At halftime, our linemen noticed that we had bloody cuts and scratches on our face, hands, and legs. We soon concluded that the other team had removed the cleats from their shoes. The sole of a football shoe has a series of screw-like spikes onto which the rubber cleats are screwed. When the cleats are on, there is little chance you will wound an opponent. Take the cleats off, however, and the effect is similar to a knife cut. We managed to win this game, but the back alley stunts both teams used were far more memorable and taught us yet another lesson on being prepared and never taking the opponent casually.

North Little Rock High School also had a B Team and we played them several times during the season because we were only a short distance from each other. Playing them so often afforded us an opportunity to get to know their players. In my case, one of their guards and I spent some long Thursday afternoons butting heads. We seemed to alternate our good days and our bad. On the last game of the season with them, my opponent and I had the same idea about what to do when the game was over.

Before leaving the field, we shook hands and introduced ourselves. His name was Billy Skipper. The simple gesture of two young men who had played hard, well, and fairly and in turn had earned their mutual respect was one of the most satisfying experiences I had during my three years in high school. What a fantastic year 1950 was! And the best was yet to come, I thought, in 1951.

Chapter 20
Gross

There is nothing in the world grosser than a teenage boy when he wants to be, or even when he doesn't know he is. Many instances could be cited, dear reader, but the worst examples must remain forever in the secure closet of memories.

In 1950, a fad developed in the school halls of directing a solid punch with a clinched fist to your friend's groin. At first the punches were somewhat restrained, although still painful. Gradually they grew in intensity. In the early stages of this fad the offender would attack only someone he knew. Then it branched out to strangers. Ultimately the practice occurred even when the target was talking to his girlfriend. The girls naturally thought we were Neanderthals. Why any of us thought this was funny will forever remain a mystery.

As a defensive measure, boys distrusted every other male within an arm's length of them. The typical defensive measure was to situate your pelvic area in a stance that put it somewhat behind the upper torso. In still other cases, the best protection was to place both hands in front of the groin, no matter how it looked.

The coaches became aware of this stupid antic and began issuing warnings to knock it off. No one was sorry to see this nonsense cease, and no one really ever knew how it started in the first place.

Regrettably I played an unwitting role in grossing Coach Matthews out. This occurred in the school cafeteria. The cafeteria, I always thought, was just a place where one buys food and consumes it, all within 30 minutes. Teachers are expected to monitor behavior in the cafeteria where they also dine.

In my lunch hour the athletes ate together at a separate table. Coach Matthews observed them while he also ate in the general vicinity. As was my habit, I would go through the cafeteria line and then place my tray on the dining table. Next I would go get a glass of water and come back to the table. Surprise! Half my food would be gone or there would be a dirty napkin in my plate, or something else would have transpired to make the meal inedible. In many cases the culprit was Charles Reed.

What to do? I tried taking my tray with me when I got the water, but this was often cumbersome. Next I tried walking sideways to get the water while keeping an eye on my tray on the table. However, this caused me to bump into people.

Then I found the ultimate solution. To keep these clowns from stealing my food, I decided to spit on it, or pretend to do so, making sure that the scavengers saw me when I did it. This proved highly effective. Alas, however, Coach Matthews observed me doing this from afar. He was not aware of what had precipitated my behavior, or how many lunches had been destroyed. All he saw, or knew, was that Cate was spitting in his food. My attempts to explain were not well received. Weeks later he would recount to others that I had exhibited the grossest behavior he had ever seen. It's a good thing he never saw some of the other things that went on.

It is quite possible that one of the really gross images was totally sanctified but was seldom observed by the outside world. This might be referred to as "twinkle toes grossness."

If you didn't have athlete's foot when you entered the 10th grade, you only had to wait a few days, and you would have it until you graduated. There really wasn't a cure for it, and it was an unsightly mess of rotting flesh between the toes, and peeling skin. Although there wasn't a cure, there was a symptomatic treatment.

Doc placed a box in the locker room that had some type of topical medicated powder in it. The routine consisted of standing in the box with your bare feet, and then applying a tar-like substance over your toes with the powder on them. The net effect was to bind the toes of the feet together for what seemed like permanently. Given an hour or so to dry, your toes were bound together for days. The front of your feet would be black and the toes were stuck together, but it worked.

Most guys wore white socks with their penny-loafers. Little did the non-athletes know or suspect what was hidden from the world—a smelly, gross, black concoction that we more or less used as long as we played football.

Chapter 21
Dating

The material in this book is so dominated by football players doing guy things, one might get the impression there were no girls in our existence. That would be both incorrect and unfortunate. Thankfully it is not true!

There were 1,500 students in Little Rock Senior High School, and roughly half of them (750) were girls. In contrast, there were only about 75 football players. As you can see, if a girl liked to date football players, the odds were not in her favor—about 10 to one against her. But, expressed more positively, the odds were 10 to

Paul Y. Griffin, Sr., president of the Little Rock School Board, gave daughter Ethel Belle Griffin her high school diploma in 1952.

one in favor of the players! There does seem to be some truth to the notion that, as a general rule, girls have an interest in football players, but that's all it is—a general rule.

Let's start out by acknowledging one important reality. When you are a sophomore, you may not have your driver's license, and therefore you have no car. This can be a serious handicap to your social life until you have a license with no restrictions as well as the use of your parents' car.

Because of the car situation, my social life in the 10th grade was relatively benign. It mainly consisted of sock hops and hayrides where transportation was not essential. Several of my

"Gold Jackets Booster Club" in 1952. Back row, left to right: Patsy Courtney, Sally McKelvey, Barbara Miller. Front row, left to right: Millicent Tesche, Ethel Belle Griffin, Carolyn Corley, Mary Lillian Lee.

player friends and I would drop in on these events, having been brought there by friends or family.

The 11th grade was a different story. In addition to being a superb season for football, one day my father brought home a brand new 1950 Oldsmobile 88! This car matched my new unrestricted driver's license very nicely, and had pickup that was so exceptional I heard some men comment they were afraid they might lose control of a machine that could reach 60 mph in 15 seconds.

With this constraint on my social life now a thing of the past, dating became more feasible, but date whom? I soon found

Gold Jackets Booster Club 50 years later. Back row, left to right: Patsy Courtney Gladden, Sally McKelvey Prickett, Barbara Miller Throneberry. Front row, left to right: Millicent Tesche Martin, Ethel Belle Griffin Curry, Carolyn Corley Steelman, Mary Lillian Lee Chaney.

that this was not a problem. More specifically, what all the young players discovered is that girls would seek them out, using their own techniques. The most common technique was for her to tell a friend to let you know that if you called her for a date the answer would be YES. Another approach was simply to bump into you. Yes, I mean bump into you like a linebacker. After doing so she would apologize for the "accident," introduce herself, and go from there.

Not too far into the school year I found myself going steady with Virginia. Still later I became a steady with Crys and Lynn, and by the 12th grade I discovered Charlotte. Somewhere in this lineup I also dated Ethel until her future husband, guard Wayland Roberts, entered the scene and took over.

One might wonder about the series of "steadies" referred to above. Why so many? The answer is that a teammate, Bill, thought my choice of girls was excellent. So excellent, in fact, that he eased me out of the picture with every one of them. With friends like Bill, who needs enemies?

Then one day, I met a girl who may have been heaven sent. Literally! My teammate Bob McFarlin was dating a girl from St. Mary's Academy in Little Rock, and she had a sister named Mary. St. Mary's was a gothic institution that was for school girls only. Bob wanted to arrange a blind date with Mary. Reluctantly I agreed. Bob definitely did me a favor. Mary was attractive and she was nice. Since she was not a student at my school, I thought I just might be able to keep Bill away from her.

On the first date we attended an affair held in St. Mary's gymnasium. Mary told me that it was important to meet some of the nuns that were there. They proved to be very friendly, even though I think the purpose of the introductions was to pass some type of test. Mary and I dated several years, and Bill never moved in on me!

Speaking of introductions, there were no introductions in those days like the ones you had to pass each time you arrived to pick up your date. It was standard operating procedure that when you arrived your date was never ready. By formula, she was always 15 minutes late. The purpose of this time gap was for you to meet her father and be cross-examined. For example, the first meeting with Ethel Griffin's father went something like this:

"Tell me about yourself. How are you doing in school? Where are you taking her tonight? Who else will be there? When will you be home?"

There was a standard repertoire that all the fathers seemed to use. Although it took me a while to play this game, I eventually learned the types of things to tell my date's parents:

"I will not speed; I have never received a traffic ticket or had an accident; I will have her home on time, if not sooner."

This was my social playbook. I lived up to my promises and eventually my parents were receiving flattering feedback on me from the parents of the girls I dated. Incidentally, here's what "being on time" meant 10:00 p.m. on Friday, 11:00 p.m. on Saturday, 8:00 p.m. on Sunday, and Monday-Thursday were never allowed.

Years later, when my own teenage daughter started dating, I told her we would follow the same routine I had to go through when I was in high school. She was appalled at the very notion! I did it only one time and after that gave it up as hopeless. I suppose times do change, and that meant that her old fuddy duddy father had to change with them. Nevertheless, I still think it wasn't a bad system.

There were several girls' organizations in our school. This included the Gold Jackets, the Hi Jinks, and, of course, the cheerleaders. They were fiercely loyal to all the school's athletic teams, but especially the football team.

In 1951, we traveled to Texarkana and were defeated. The trip back home took several hours, and we arrived around 2:00 a.m. As we got off the bus, to our surprise, the cheerleaders were waiting for us and applauded as each player stepped out. Lila Matthews was one of them, and she is forever framed in my memory because of her untimely death in a car accident a few years later.

Chapter 22
Report Cards

Most kids with bad report cards only had to deal with their parents. If you were a football player, you first had to deal with the coaches. On the day report cards were out, we were required to give them to Coach Matthews. The coaches would look at the cards together and their reactions were usually loud and animated.

One grading period in 1950, showed I had mostly "C's" and "D's." I did, however, have one "A." This singular mark of distinction was in English. All three coaches looked at the report card in disbelief. I could hear them comment on it 10 yards away. Then began the interrogation.

"How in the hell did you get an "A" in English?"

"Did you borrow somebody else's work?"

"Is this a mistake?"

Finally they gave it up, much to my relief.

I have no recollection of any member of our team ever losing eligibility because of grades, and I do believe that Coach Matthews and his assistants genuinely cared that their boys performed well academically. However, if a crystal ball told them that Cate would eventually become a tenured Assistant Professor of Economics, they never would have believed it, and I doubt that I would have either.

A cursory analysis of the team of 1951, as an example, would reveal that perhaps a disproportionate number of them went on to great careers in their private lives. Henry Moore and Paul Goad eventually played in the NFL—Henry for the Giants and Paul for the 49ers. (As the Giant's Number One NFL draft pick, Henry received the princely signing bonus of $500). Several other players such as Billy Hastings and Tom Blagg played college football on scholarships. Bob MacFarlin became a doctor. Bill Barnhouse played football for Henderson State Teachers College and eventually became a high school principal in Little Rock. Lacy Frazer became a doctor and practiced in Little Rock (and attended to my mother shortly before she died); Harold Meeks had a long career in public relations with a major corporation, and was instrumental in sustaining Wilson's Tigers.

M.L. Stephens earned his Ph.D. and was a university professor, as was Jim Wallace. John Cochran became head coach of a high school in Kansas. Winston Porter managed a savings and loan institution in Alabama. Still other members of the team became professional soldiers and businessmen.

One member of the '51 team, Charles Reed, perhaps merits special attention for an exemplary career after football. He played for Hendrix College and then entered the U.S. Navy where he became a helicopter pilot on a carrier based in the Philippines. He subsequently moved to Houston, Texas.

Charles Reed became a pioneer in expanding and teaching in the new field of cardiovascular perfusion. Prior to the early fifties, it was not possible to operate on the heart. After Dr. John Gibbons invented a new medical device called the heart-lung machine, open-heart surgery became possible for the first time. This machine assumed the function of the human heart while immobilized during invasive surgery. Blood from the patient's body was channeled to the heart-lung machine where it was cleansed and recirculated to the body. This support device kept the patient alive until the surgery was over and the patient's heart could resume its normal functioning. The individual who operates the heart-lung machine is a highly skilled medical person known as a *perfusionist*.

Reed went to Texas Heart Institute in Houston and worked for the world-famous thoracic surgeon, Dr. Denton Cooley. Recognizing that perfusion was in its infancy, Charles led an effort to set up one of the nation's early programs to train perfusionists and to develop standards of practice. Of monumental importance, he and a colleague, Ms. Diane Clark, wrote the first textbook that attempted to set forth a body of knowledge for the practice of perfusion. They later led an effort to establish a program to certify perfusionists. The certification program to this day is the internationally recognized standard of perfusionist credentialing.

There are approximately 20 academic programs in the United States that train perfusionists. Each year hundreds of thousands of open-heart surgery cases are performed, including those for infants. Open-heart surgery is not possible without the heart-lung machine and the perfusionists who operate it. (The Arkansas Children's Hospital in Little Rock is one of the most prestigious institutions in the world performing open-heart surgery for infants and children.)

Charlie, as we called him, was the son of a prominent Little Rock doctor. Tragically, his father died when Charlie was in the 11th grade. His funeral was extraordinarily well attended, surrounded by the pomp and circumstance of the Masonic temple to which he belonged. Charlie's ambition was to become a doctor as well, but instead his career led him down the road of becoming a world authority on cardiovascular perfusion.

Interestingly, Charlie took on many characteristics of the Wilson Matthews persona. Although he died a young man, the older he became the more his personality resembled Coach Matthews. He once told me that, while in the Navy, he watched helplessly as a friend burned to death in a plane crash. This affected him, and, in his subsequent career in perfusion, he gained a reputation for being hard-bitten, short-tempered, and very intolerant of mistakes. However, as in the case of Coach Matthews, Charlie had another side to him that was rather private. He published several volumes of poetry, and periodically he hacked through the jungles of Costa Rica in search of new varieties of orchids.

The 25th reunion of the Class of '52 honored Coach Matthews. All of his former players greeted him with salutations such as "Hello Coach" or "Hi Coach." It was always "Coach" something. And then along came Charlie.

"Hi, Wilson, it's good to see you," Charlie said. Coach didn't exactly smile at this greeting, but he did give Charlie a good handshake. The onlookers at this little exchange held their breath, but if Coach took offense he didn't show it. Another plausible interpretation is that Coach did not resent being greeted in this fashion because he was proud of what Charlie had become as a man.

With Coach Matthews and his staff, football was important, but it was not so important as to take precedence over academics. The shelf life of high school football is three years. The shelf life of an education is forever. They tried to convey this to us simply by making sure our report cards showed we had our priorities in order.

It is understandable that coaches are preoccupied with producing football players. That's their job. But as they grow older, it surely must start to impress them what their boys become in later life. As Brian Cox might put it, it's the Pride of the Tigers.

Chapter 23
The Tradition

A tradition of long standing was the annual scrimmage between the A Team and the B Team. This event was always held late in the season. Strangely, the B Team often won this game. For this reason, the Varsity players always took this game very seriously. My recollection of the 1950 scrimmage is telescoped to one series of plays when the B Team was on offense.

After leaving the huddle and positioning myself on the line, I found the opposition staring at me across the line was my best friend Eddie Bradford, and Carl Slaughter. By 1950 Eddie was all-everything. By the season's end he was named National High School All-American, and played in their game in Memphis in 1951.

Carl Slaughter was also well known as a player, but in my book he was tremendously underrated. The only people who under-rated Carl were those who never played against him. Carl had red hair and a lean muscular body. I never saw him when he didn't have blood on the top of his nose. Personality-wise, Carl was a gentleman's gentleman. He was soft spoken, genuinely polite, and gracious, up to a point. The point when he underwent a psychological transformation was when he stepped on the football field. Of all Carl's football skills, his ability to charge the offense like a cannonball was simply amazing.

So here I was, looking at two extraordinary players who were going to attack me the instant the center snapped the ball. Which is what happened.

On the first play I tried making my best possible block. All I remember was darkness. Did I block either one of them? No way;

not even close. In fact, I really didn't know what happened on the play. I was buried on the line of scrimmage.

Next play. This time I was determined to succeed. This time I would block them lower than before. The result was even worse, as I arose from the ground and tried to clear my head. I tried several adjustments, but to no avail. Block 'em high, block 'em low, cross block 'em, it made no difference. Then I received a final greeting, when Carl and Eddie hit me so hard I became a cartoon character.

In cartoons when someone is hit the artist always draws stars above the character's head to illustrate how hard the blow was. Until this scrimmage, I always thought that cartoon stars were just make-believe. However, Carl and my old friend Eddie actually proved to me that you can see stars if you're hit hard enough.

Fifty years later, I had occasion to visit an Ear, Nose, and Throat physician about my nose. I complained to the doctor that I was having trouble breathing through my nose. After examining me and taking x-rays, he casually commented, "Of course I guess you know you have a broken nose." The instant he said this my mind had a flashback to that 1950 scrimmage when Carl and Eddie left their calling card on my nose. Thanks guys!

Carl Slaughter went on to become a doctor, and Eddie Bradford became a career army officer in the medical corps. I'd like to think that their choice of careers in the medical field were intended as atonement for all the injured (no, make that hurt) on football fields in Arkansas and surrounding states for which they were responsible!

Chapter 24
The Bitter Lesson

When the first period study hall class met for the first time in September, Coach Matthews surveyed their faces and then called me forward.

"Would you like to be in charge whenever I'm not here?"

"Yes sir," was my instant reply.

Little did I know that he was almost never there, and that I was literally in charge most of the time. My duties were simple—check the roster, report the people who were absent, and maintain order. With regard to order, there was almost never any problem.

One day, a member of the class approached me to ask if he could be excused for some personal business. I knew him from junior high school and told him okay. A few days later he came to me with the same request, which I again agreed to. More requests followed until it reached the point that he no longer bothered to ask.

His absences came to a screeching halt late in the year when a staff member observed him on the street nearby and asked if he had permission to be out of school, which naturally he did not.

Coach Matthews was informed, and the next event was an invitation to me to visit Coach in his office. I had been to his office on no more than two previous occasions. Each time he was on the telephone. Judging from his end of the conversation, it was my impression Coach was selling athletic equipment to coaches at other schools. In any case, this definitely was not the subject of my latest visit.

"You know this guy, David?" he asked.

"Yes sir, I do."

"Did you mark him present when he wasn't in class?"

"Yes sir, I did."

"Well why did you do that? Didn't you understand that your job was important and that I trusted you?" he asked.

"Coach, I just wasn't thinking straight. I'm very sorry about this"

"Well, you're no longer in charge of the study hall."

Walking back to the study hall, my mind was flooded with self-condemnations. What in the world had I been thinking, letting David skip class? Of all people to do this to, Coach Matthews should have been the last person on earth! Can't you see that what you did was dishonest? Can't you now see that your friend betrayed you and that your betrayal of Coach Matthews began the first time you let David skip class? Why is it that an obvious choice between right and wrong totally escaped you? Stupid, stupid, stupid!

These types of questions pursued me all day. Fortunately, we would have our typical winter football practice outdoors this afternoon, and maybe I could get my mind off my sins.

After assembling on the practice field, Coach routinely called for the first team of the varsity to line up. I was proud beyond words to be the right guard, which meant I would likely be a starter for the 1951 season. As we took our positions on the line of scrimmage, Coach calmly called me to withdraw. He then appointed my replacement.

In the spirited competition for positions, there was often very little difference between candidates. There were several other young men who were fully capable of playing right guard. Until this day, the position appeared to have been mine, but now, no more. I was no longer the starting right guard, and I could only hope I might be again.

Day after day I bombarded myself with recriminations. How could you have jeopardized everything you worked so hard for just so a guy could skip class? Stupid, stupid, stupid! As each day of practice came and went, I became an onlooker more than anything else. A darn substitute! For my lapse in judgment, I might finish my career as a "sub." When you aren't trustworthy, this is what happens.

Chapter 25
Try Again

I resolved that on August 20, 1951, I would be in the best possible physical condition. This ambition was shared by my friends and teammates, Dick Gladden, Ed Rutledge, John Cochran, William Bell, and Bob McFarlin.

If I were to be given another chance to regain my starting guard position, I was dedicated to the goal that I would be superbly prepared for the opportunity. This resolve also had a spiritual side to it. Rev. Vaught baptized me one summer evening in the baptismal (total immersion was required) of the church. Hopefully, this gave me a new start, I thought. At least for now, I was spiritually born again.

Throughout the summer of '51, our little group would meet from time to time to work out, and work we did. Running up the stairs of Tiger stadium, grass drills, gassers, push ups, sit-ups … you name it, we did it, and in abundance. Our bodies became strong and brown from the sun, and our lung capacity and leg strength were the best ever. Each time we met we worked even harder until we far exceeded anything we would be asked to do when practice began on August 20.

Shortly before August 20, there was one last ritual to perform. In addition to running up the stadium stairs and performing all the traditional exercises, there were two other final crowning achievements to accomplish.

The first was to lie down in the south end zone of Tiger Stadium and roll over and over for the hundred yards to the north end zone. At the end of this undertaking, we would stand up, regain our balance, and proceed to throw up. If you didn't throw up that meant you hadn't worked hard enough.

Shortly thereafter, the second undertaking was to run 20 laps around the stadium track. This was approximately five miles and it was run in the middle of the day when the sun bore down without mercy.

The last lap was rather like a victory lap. When it was finished you knew you were ready for the final season. Let the games begin!

Chapter 26
New Hope

The summer of 1951 was brutal. Our days of practice took place in temperatures of 104 degrees and sky-high humidity. One day Coach gave us three breaks (water was never allowed) and then chastised us for being the only Tiger team in history that ever took three breaks in one day. As usual, and right on schedule, someone would ask him if we would practice on Labor Day, and of course the questioner received the customary answer with the customary snarl.

By the end of training camp absolutely nothing had changed in my situation. I was still on the second team. While getting dressed after the final practice, a student manager told me Coach wanted to see me in his office. "Oh boy" I thought, "the other shoe is about to drop."

"Come in, George" Coach greeted me. "I wanted to tell you that the coaches thought you had a good camp and that you can help us be a better team this fall."

"Wow." I thought, "There may be hope for me yet."

"But," he continued, "I don't think you have much chance of lettering."

"Yes sir. I'll try to help the team any way I can."

"Okay, George, just so long as you know that your chances of lettering are slim."

Back at my locker, I replayed Coach's every word. He didn't say I wouldn't letter, he just said it wasn't likely. But wait a minute! Things can happen! Guys get injured or under-perform. You never know. You just never know. I've still got a chance …. I've still got an outside chance!

Chapter 27
Polio

Polio. In 1951, no five-letter word struck more fear in the public's mind than Polio. There was no cure, and the outcome, assuming you lived, was usually paralysis of the legs requiring heavy metal braces and crutches. In some cases, the outcome was so bad the patient had to live in an iron lung in order to breathe.

Public health authorities didn't know what to do when an epidemic occurred. Mainly they tried to keep people from congregating. Accordingly, public swimming pools were closed as well as movie houses. Polio, however, did not curtail our daily football practice.

There were some players that Coach Matthews was always after in practice. They were usually linemen, and they were accustomed to receiving verbal reprimands. As an example, one day in scrimmage a left tackle pulled to the right to execute a trap play. However, the right tackle pulled to the left to execute the trap play. The left tackle was wrong. The result was that they had a violent collision right behind the center, with blood flowing freely from the left tackle's face. He had been knocked silly. Coach looked at the player who was bleeding and uttered the famous words "Hurts don't it?" This was then followed by a tirade regarding the price of stupidity if you don't know your plays.

Backs were seldom criticized, and I doubt that our quarterback, Ted Bellingrath, was ever openly corrected. On the other hand, he didn't make many mistakes. It was unusual for halfback Ed Goldman to be on the receiving end of negative comments from Coach Matthews. It was a delight to watch Ed run, especially on plays into the middle of the line. He was as quick as they came, and his trademark was to holler out to Ted "Hey, gimmie that pill" just before taking a handoff and crashing into the line.

Ed wasn't the type of player a coach had to ride. He had a strong work ethic. Thus it was noteworthy that lately Coach Matthews had been on Ed's case about not running hard and not running his routes as far as he should have. One afternoon in class, Ethel Griffin noticed Ed wasn't feeling well.

"Ed, you ought to see the school nurse or a doctor. You don't look well."

"No, I'll be alright." But he wasn't.

That night Ed was admitted to the hospital. Diagnosis: Polio.

For the next few weeks the practice field atmosphere was subdued. Ed's illness hung over us like a cloud. Ed was sick, and there was nothing that we could do for him. Kinda' like Riley Johns.

Eventually, Coach said we could visit Ed in the hospital. When we did so, we discovered he was attended by an English nurse, and she was a real cheer leader. She constantly told Ed he looked great and was getting better.

But Ed Goldman, one of the nicest young men you could ever know, a nifty little halfback who had a great personality, was not getting better. His lifetime sentence was iron braces, and he never walked again without them. This was a sad ending for a young man who wanted to play for Princeton. One night before a game, Coach Matthews referred to Ed, and then choked up. We understood.

Like the champion that he was, Ed went on to have a successful business career later in life.

SENIOR YEAR

Chapter 28
The Livestock Show

The 1951 season got off to a superb start. The Tigers notched wins early on against major teams from other states. Coach Steed White, who had just replaced Howard Pearce as the line coach, was overheard advising Coach Matthews that our team was so good he wouldn't make us scrimmage anymore this season, so as to keep our legs fresh.

The team certainly agreed with Coach White, not that that carried any particular weight. However, we did believe that our performance was worthy enough to merit a Monday afternoon off to go to the Arkansas Livestock Show. For some reason, attending this event was a big deal, notwithstanding that as city boys we hardly knew the difference between a Hereford and a Guernsey.

Our plans, however, were soon dashed as the word came down from on high that we would practice that day as usual. Forget the Livestock Show. Early that afternoon we ran the 50 yards from the school to the stadium. This was the required way to go to practice. Some time in the past, Coach Matthews had observed us straggling our way from the school to the stadium and somehow got the outlandish impression that our speed and our demeanor seemed more characteristic of people who were not enthusiastic about coming to practice.

Accordingly, that very day he laid down a new rule, which was that the minute we left the school we were to start running and not stop until we arrived at the stadium. This was why we ran today, when we really wanted to be elsewhere. Frequently thereafter he could be seen monitoring our compliance with this new edict.

Against all reason, we wondered if maybe practice would be shorter than usual, thus still allowing us a chance to attend the show. We couldn't have been more wrong. For most of us, we were about to experience the most brutal day of football we would ever have as long as we played.

Practice began with a basic scrimmage. Running backs straight up the middle. Linemen blocking straight ahead. Over and over and over again. One hour passed. Then two hours passed. This had become what is known as smash mouth football. The hot Arkansas sun became hotter, as did our tempers.

The plays we ran were not new nor did they have any finesse. We began to wonder what the purpose of this was. Still the practice continued. The day was now extremely hot—skirmishes began to break out even among friends.

During this scene Coach had little to say. He stood silently, almost like a spectator. Finally he commented that if anyone wanted to quit the team they were welcome to do so.

Suddenly, in an electric moment, a player who was a starter and highly respected announced "I quit." He headed toward the locker room, but before he got very far, another player of equal stature grabbed him and dragged him back to the field. "You're not quitting," he hollered.

More plays were run. By now most of the players had blood or scrapes on their face and hands. Noses were the most common area affected. Suddenly, another player walked off the field. It was the same person who had earlier talked his teammate into not quitting, and incredibly, the friend he had helped now talked him into returning.

Now, almost as if a mutiny were occurring, still other players quit and were in turn brought back. During all this pandemonium, Coach Matthews looked on silently. Only occasionally would he say, "Anyone can leave that wants to."

Finally the practice ended. When it was over, no one had quit for good. Bloody, sweaty, dehydrated, and totally exhausted, we trailed back to the locker room. To heck with the Livestock Show. Who wants to go now anyway?

To this day the players do not understand the dynamics of that afternoon. What was the point? What was he trying to accomplish? Were we now better than we were? We didn't know then nor do we now.

Chapter 29
Public Relations

On one of our road trips the home team fans rode the Tigers without mercy. As the night went on, the jeers from the fans were directed more toward Coach Matthews. Each time our team made a mistake or played poorly, the boo birds directed their insults and catcalls to Coach.

Finally, Coach had had enough. After one particularly harsh insult, he turned around from the playing field and stared at the crowd. Suddenly he raised his hand and showed them his middle finger. I was very close to him when he did this, and I thought to myself that this is going to start something really big.

To the contrary, however, the crowd uttered not a word. In fact, there were no other jibes from the stands during the rest of the game.

You are probably aware that the name of the athletic teams of the University of Tennessee is "Volunteers," but have you ever heard of the Central Volunteers? Probably not!

Occasionally at the end of a practice, Coach Matthews would call us around him before we went to the locker room. This was usually a pretty good sign that he had volunteered the team to take part in some civic activity. One afternoon he announced he was looking for volunteers to help with the downtown merchants' Christmas parade (similar to Macy's annual event).

Predictably, newcomers to the squad would ask all the questions, e.g., how much is the pay, are we served dinner, will we get out of football practice, will transportation be provided, etc. In short, all the wrong questions. Never mind, however, because the questions weren't going to be answered anyway. Coach's adjutant general, Eddie Bradford, was in charge of Q and A. Eddie would seek the questioners out and dress them down for poor attitudes. The answer to all their questions was NO, end of session.

So, a few nights later, the Tigers were carrying balloon floats down Main Street. Poorly dressed because of unusually cold weather, we did our duty, even on empty stomachs. The parade was a success, the merchants were happy, the parade crowds were excited, and goodwill abounded for those "volunteers" from Central.

A similar request for volunteers came a few months later when the weather was warm again. This time it was to help downtown merchants collect paper. The project they had in mind, however, was a little more ambitious than we thought. We understood our mission to be going to the sidewalk in front of each store and business and loading the bundled paper materials into a truck for transportation to the disposal facility. An intermediate step was missing however. The merchants expected us to do the bundling. More specifically, our job was to go into their places of business and do all the sorting and binding, after which the materials could be taken to the sidewalk where we would then load them in the truck. This was a major effort and required us to work late that day to finish our work. The merchants, however, were gratified at the volunteers' efforts.

While the volunteers griped about these projects, the more mature recognized that our City did a lot for its kids, especially for the high school. What we accomplished was good for the team and reflected well on Coach Matthews.

In a pre-game ceremony at the Thanksgiving Day game with North Little Rock High School, Coach Matthews was given a new car. As a whole, his public relations seemed to be in pretty good shape.

Chapter 30
Nothing To Celebrate

Late in the season we had an away game with Fort Smith. Things did not go well in the early stages of this game. Not unexpectedly, Coach Matthews berated us at halftime for our poor performance. In the second half, however, we turned things around, and in the end we won the game by a substantial margin.

After the game, we slowly began to board our bus. Coach Steed White also boarded, and, as he proceeded down the aisle, he engaged some of the boys in good-natured banter about how tough they thought they were. He and two of the players started a little rough housing, all in good humor. Suddenly a voice from the front of the bus blasted out.

"You got nothing to be proud of tonight—sit down and shut up!" It was Coach Matthews.

Coach White attempted to explain to Coach Matthews that they were just playing around. To the embarrassment of the players, Coach then reprimanded Coach White.

The trip home to Little Rock was very quiet. Players wondered what had turned so sour. Was it because we didn't have a lead from the very beginning? Did we not win by a large enough score? No one knew. This was one game where it was hard to tell the difference between winning and losing.

In the days that followed, Coach appeared to be under stress. While privately noting that he thought this '51 team might be the best he ever had, it didn't appear that way to the players. The level of harassment seemed to be increasing. Then one day it hit me, both literally and figuratively.

In a practice session one afternoon, Coach wanted to experiment with playing offensive linemen "tight" and "loose." Playing tight meant that the linemen would physically touch each other side-by-side in their line of scrimmage alignment, leaving no gaps. Playing loose meant there were varying degrees of distance between them, e.g., six inches, eight inches, etc.

While on the line of scrimmage and facing downfield, Coach said something to me. I thought he said to move in tighter, and I did so. Then he said something else to me, which I further construed to move in even more. I was incorrect on both counts.

While continuing to face downfield, I suddenly felt myself propelled head over heel for at least five feet. I did not fully comprehend what had happened. Belatedly I realized Coach had kicked me. Turning around to face him, I beheld the most unusual sight. There was Coach Matthews hobbling around on his left foot while holding his right foot and moaning with pain.

"Cate," he screamed, "if I've broken my foot you're off the team!"

Practice was soon declared over. In the hours remaining before the start of school the next day, I could only wonder if his foot was broken and if my playing days were over.

The next day I arrived at school early. I positioned myself in a spot near the parking lot where I could see Coach when he parked his car. He arrived on schedule in his blue Pontiac, opened the door, and eased his way out, and he had a very noticeable limp! That's it, I thought. I'll get the word soon.

I did not appreciate that this incident had taken on a life of its own. Whereas I regarded it as my personal problem, the entire team had become fascinated with it, and even some of the students who were not athletes. I wasn't the only one who could hardly wait for Coach to arrive.

For some unknown reason, he never raised the issue of a broken foot. In fact, it was not broken, but it must have felt to him as if it were. Decades later, every time I attend a class reunion, guys come up to me and ask if I remember the kicking incident. It is astonishing that they think I may have forgotten it. If it weren't the kick heard 'round the world, it was at least the kick that was heard 'round Tiger Stadium.

Chapter 31
First Five Minutes

In 1951, the tradition of winning was so established in the culture of Little Rock Senior High School, there was no acceptable alternative. You either won or else.

Coach Matthews was not big on making pre-game locker room speeches. He mainly used the time to review with us the major points of our strategy. However, there was one ritual we followed every game, and it emanated from the players, not unlike what one would witness at a church revival.

"First five minutes!" someone would holler. "

"Yeah, that's right, first five minutes!" someone else would add.

Quickly in unison, everyone shouted, "First five minutes!"

Almost on cue, Coach Matthews would shout, "That's right boys, first five minutes. Go out there and pop it to them in the first five minutes. Let them know they're going to lose this game just like every other year they played us. And remember this, boys: you've got the momentum because of the great Tiger teams that played before you. Don't let'em down!"

When the time drew near to take the field, we left the locker room and gathered in a hallway that led to the field. The locker room of the guest team faced ours, and their players were assembled in the same area. This provided us with the opportunity to make smart remarks about how they were going to lose and get trampled in this game. The appropriate word to describe what was going on was *intimidation*, and it seemed to work.

One of the many reasons why Wilson Matthews was so successful was his attention to detail. It was legendary. A good example is how he treated the visiting teams.

One day in 1949, the word went out that all the football players should meet in the school auditorium. No subject was announced. Once gathered, he announced that the visiting team from Tennessee had arrived and he met their bus and coach. He greeted the visitors so cordially they must have thought he had a Welcome Wagon franchise. He also observed their players as they left the bus. The visiting coach was impressed and appreciative that Coach Matthews had been so kind as to meet the bus and assist them in getting settled for the game. Coach then made a beeline to the school auditorium to meet with the team.

What followed next was nothing less than a scouting report. He had scrutinized each player getting off the bus ... height, weight, build, and demeanor. He then told us that some of their players were tall and had big bony knees, and therefore we would need to tackle them higher than we normally would. So it went, taking a multitude of seemingly innocuous observations and translating them into a scouting report. The Tennessee team was soundly defeated.

If Coach ever used a ploy to motivate a team, it was often to hold up a great former player as an example. One week we were scheduled to play Istrouma High School from Baton Rouge, Louisiana. Istrouma was a highly regarded team, but fortunately Coach Matthews appeared to have a scouting report. Before practice one day, he gathered us around to listen to a letter he had received from Larry Jones, who graduated in 1951, and who now played for Louisiana State University, also located in Baton Rouge. Larry's letter was the scouting report.

Larry had watched Istrouma practice and listed their strengths and weaknesses in unemotional and clinical detail. At the end of his letter, however, he commented that we could win this game if we hitched up our guts and carried the fight to them. Be rough and tough and you can win was the message, short and simple.

When Coach finished reading the letter, he slapped it with his right hand and yelled out, "That's just like ole Larry! He never was afraid to stick his head in where things are tough! He knows how we can win! I thank God I've had players like ole Larry. You boys know Larry and you know he's right! Just be tough!" The next Friday night we beat Istrouma by one point.

On another occasion, Coach was discussing the defensive backfield of an upcoming opponent.

"They have this one defensive back that you can handle okay. All you need to do is …"

"Put a shoulder in his gut" Billy Hastings interrupted.

"That's right, but how did you know?"

"We learned that about him last year when we played them. Give him a good hit and he's no problem."

Coach's smile and expression showed Billy's unrehearsed and spontaneous remark pleased him immensely.

Chapter 32
The Rinky Dinks

What is a Rinky Dink?

Search me. I don't know, except I suspect it isn't very flattering. In any event, there were a half dozen or so substitute players that Coach Matthews referred to this way, and I was one of them.

The Rinky Dinks seldom played until the score was hopelessly beyond the opposing team's ability to recover. When he decided it was safe to relieve the regulars with us, he would typically admonish us, "Alright you Rinky Dinks, get out there and don't screw up." The first time he said this in a game, the moniker "Rinky Dinks" became a badge of honor to us.

What often happened was that the Rinky Dinks were so glad to get in a game, and because they weren't tired, they continued to run up the score on the opposition. During the 1951 season the Rinky Dinks probably played in at least a half dozen games, but we had no impact on the overall record of nine wins and three losses.

The Rinky Dinks did, however, have a special role to play, largely unbeknownst to anyone else, even now. We discovered we were just a bunch of pretty faces.

In the Homecoming game and the Thanksgiving Day game, there were halftime ceremonies. As usual, pretty girls were paraded to the center of the field, escorted of course by football players. Had the fans paid closer attention, however, they might have detected that the girls' player escorts were not the stars of the team. No, they were the Rinky Dinks!

The architect of this arrangement was Coach Matthews. Why? The answer is that during halftime he wanted his starting players in the locker room where he could discuss changes in strategy and develop new plans for the second half. The last place he wanted them was participating in escort services.

However, the Rinky Dinks almost succeeded in making the ceremonies a fiasco. There had been no rehearsal of our role as escorts. The result was that somehow there were fewer escorts than there were princesses to escort off the field. Joan Rule was standing close to me and she realized to her horror what was transpiring.

"George Cate," she said, "Don't you dare leave me alone out here in front of all these people." I extended my arm to Joan and off the field we walked. However, I believe one of the Rinky Dinks had to make a second trip to midfield to retrieve a stranded princess. Nevertheless, we had done our duty. Several weeks later, in an official ceremony in the school auditorium, the Rinky Dinks would receive formal recognition for their contribution to the 1951 season.

Chapter 33
Closure

The 1951 Tigers won nine games and lost three, but unlike their predecessors, they did not win the conference championship. Thus, in all our eyes, it was a total failure. Perhaps worst of all, we were defeated 14-13 by North Little Rock in the annual Thanksgiving Day game. Back in our locker room after the game was over, we simply sat in stunned silence. The inconceivable had just happened, and it was beyond belief. The atmosphere in the locker room was akin to a funeral. We should have won this game and we should have won the championship, but we didn't. And now we were getting a large dose of loser's medicine.

Finally the silence was broken by tackle Bob McFarlin. Bob's taped hands covered his face and he was in great despair. He was not alone.

"Coach, we're sorry," he cried out ...

"I know, Bob, but it's too late now for that," Coach Matthews said softly.

Coach Matthews' detractors probably expected to hear that he had a temper tantrum over this loss. The facts are, however, that he comforted the boys and, if anything, lowered his voice. There was no ranting or raving from this man who hated to lose worse than anything. In this final game for the seniors he had taught them one last lesson, which was how to lose with class. In our eyes he never looked as good as he did that afternoon in the locker room. There was a time to get ready to play football, and that was months ago in the hot Arkansas sun. That was the appropriate occasion for ventilating and pushing these young men to their physical limits and beyond.

As we slowly left the stadium, the North Little Rock fans lingered. When they spotted us they taunted us. It had been years since they'd won this Thanksgiving game, so it was understandable.

The 1951 season, which could have been glorious, instead left a stigma. The team picture was hung on the auditorium wall with all the team pictures of the past. The 1951 team's picture was the only one in recent years that did not identify itself as a championship team.

A few days after the season's end, I went to the stadium to clean out my locker for the final time. On the way out, I encountered Coach Matthews.

"Hi, George. Glad I ran into you. I'm trying to decide who earned their letters this year, and I need to know how many quarters you played."

I was unprepared for this question, but nevertheless tried to remember the teams we played, when we played them, and whether I got in the game. This was a mistake on my part.

"Do you mean to tell me you don't even remember who we played this season?" he shouted. "Why the hell did I even bother to ask?"

My attempts to explain what I was doing only made matters worse. He wasn't buying my explanation and continuing to do so only made matters worse. I was relieved when he stormed away.

A few weeks later the team members gathered on the stage of the auditorium to receive their jackets with the coveted football letter on them. The jackets were piled on a table and slowly disappeared as each player stepped forward to receive it. Finally, all the jackets were gone and my name, among several, had not been called.

Coach Matthews then told the audience that he had special recognition for a particular group of players. The group he was talking about was the Rinky Dinks, although he didn't refer to us this way.

"These boys have worked very hard for three years, and although they did not play enough to earn a letter, they deserve some recognition for their service."

As our names were called, we came forth to receive a gold sweater with a football letter on it. Emblazoned on the letter was an R, standing for Reserve. As each Rinky Dink accepted his sweater, the applause was polite and scattered.

The Rinky Dinks seldom wore their sweaters. I wore mine possibly two times. Today it lies in my bureau drawer. I have never regarded it as anything other than a sign of failure. Yet there are times when I believe that Coach Matthews was trying his very best to give the recipients something to remember without compromising the standards required to earn a jacket and letter. I wish we might have had a chance to talk about this after we were both old men.

A few days later, the team attended the annual appreciation luncheon held in its honor by a local civic group. The location was in a small ballroom in the LaFayette Hotel. We wondered how this would go, given that we were not state champions this year. We all, including Coach Matthews, looked grim as we took our seats around the table.

Coach then proceeded to describe the year and expressed regrets that our record was not good enough to be a champion. Then he abandoned this negative note by ending his remarks with the statement that "In my mind, all these young men are champions." As the crowd roundly applauded, his presentation ended his responsibility to the boys of the '51 team, and he knew that from this point on, we were on our own.

Like every class before us, our own Waterloos were waiting. Some were military, some medical, some economic, and some intensely personal. M. L. Stephens, Charles Reed, Ted Bellingrath, Dub Johnson, Ed Goldman, Bill Barnhouse, Bill Kumpuris, Winston Porter, and Paul Goad all died too young, but accomplished a lot in the time they had. Even the Rinky Dinks turned out okay.

As it happens, we discovered that football was something we played while learning life's lessons. There are, of course, other ways to have accomplished this, but football, even for a substitute, wasn't too bad. Coach taught us a very important lesson that most of us have used many times. He understood that the difference between winning and losing could sometimes be an extremely small margin. In football or basketball, the difference may be one point. Think about that—one point!

The 1951 Tigers needed three points more to beat Pine Bluff and two points more to beat North Little Rock. Had these five points been scored, Little Rock would have been state champion. As it turned out, we finished third. In track, in swimming, and horseracing the difference between the winner and losers may be only a fraction of a second. A fraction of a second!

Coming close doesn't count. The difference between winning and losing is sometimes so small, the outcome is determined by who paid the most attention to detail. Attention to detail means there is nothing that is unimportant. You can fail because of one stupid seemingly insignificant thing that you didn't do well, like carry out your blocking assignment—like blocking a punt.

In the heat of competition, especially when it is literally a matter of life and death, there will be no time to talk things over before taking action. A coach understands this, which is why coaches sometimes act like dictators. There isn't time to explain things. There isn't time to get everyone's opinion before acting. Surgeons understand this, airline pilots understand this, and high school football players must understand this. Knowing the right thing to do must become instinctive.

Like keeping true attendance records.

Chapter 34
It's Over

It was raining hard now. Time to go, but was it over? You just relived three years of your life as a kid; are you going to leave it here or are you going to take this back to Virginia with the rest of your baggage?

The kid who played football here doesn't exist any more. That kid could run up the stadium stairs and run laps and do all kinds of exercises—and he could block and tackle. But he doesn't exist anymore. He's been replaced by a broken down old man with Parkinson's Disease. A good day for him is not to fall down.

You didn't earn a letter because you didn't meet the standards. You didn't meet the standard of being trustworthy, and you didn't meet the standard of playing enough quarters. So how long are you going to keep the gold sweater with the R on it in your bureau drawer?

Funny thing, over the next 20 years you met Wilson Matthews many times in the guise of graduate school professors and army sergeants and corporate division heads. He also appeared as a minister and a senior government official. Yet because of the intangibles you were taught by the original Wilson Matthews, you succeeded well with his imitators.

Now you understand that although you were a substitute player (some would say "scrub"), football was just a means to an end, and the end was to be prepared for the rough and tumble game of life. Viewed that way, you didn't do so badly.

Yes, it's over, it's finally over.

"TIGERS"
1961

Epilogue

Good Ground

Two Union generals viewed the Gettysburg panorama before the battle.

"Is this good ground?" one asked. "Yes," the other replied, "It is very good ground." What was meant by "good," one may ask? To the generals the meaning was *good* for fields of fire, *good* for defense, and *good* for victory. Most assuredly they were not referring to the beauty of the land or the fertility of the soil.

What is an American football field? It is a tract of land 60 feet wide and 300 feet long, divided into 10 equal sections of 10 yards each. The practice fields are usually even larger than this. What about the football practice field of Little Rock Central High School? Is it Good Ground?

Let me stand on the hill overlooking the field and consider this question.

Is it Good Ground? Well, for starters I know the ground is very hard and it is difficult to grow grass on it. I know that it always has small pebbles on it that the players have to remove periodically in a sweep of the field. And, oh yes, I remember that there were times when we were looking for pebbles, and we found teeth.

Of course, year in and year out the ground was splattered with the blood of the players. Maybe we should go ahead and mention sweat and other body fluids as well. And we needn't be ashamed to admit that tears sometimes fell on this ground. Are these things the ingredients of Good Ground? No, for to dwell on them is to look in the wrong place for what makes Good Ground.

The 19th Century economist David Ricardo postulated that the value of land was based on what the land produces. Land, he said, has no inherent value unto itself. If it produces wheat, however, that's a different story.

Consider the plains of West Point. Are they Good Ground? Think about the words to the West Point song:

Grip hands with the never-ending line
As we of the Corps have done,
For the men of the Corps are treading
Where they of the Corps have trod.

> (Based on lyrics to "The Corps"
> composed by Bishop Herbert S. Shipman,
> Chaplain, USMC, 1903)

The plains serve as a parade ground, but they provide a visual reminder that the Long Gray Line is the fruit of this good ground, this line that included Lee, Custer, Grant, MacArthur, Patton, Bradley, Eisenhower, Schwarzkopf, Clark, and Petraeus.

Let's open Brian Cox's book *Tiger Pride*, an outstanding piece of scholarship and research.

The place to begin is the Tiger team of 1904, which Brian says is the first recorded season. Examine the team picture. You don't see big bruisers, nor do you see many mature young men. No, what you see are little boys, almost childlike in their demeanor. One wonders what they were thinking when the picture was made. Did they have any inkling America would enter a world war while they were still in their twenties? In this new 20th Century, what were their dreams?

What did they think each August when football practice began? Were they nervous or unsure of themselves? Were they trying to impress their parents, a girlfriend, or a buddy? Were they scared but too brave to let it show?

Continue on. Wouldn't you like to reach out over the past one hundred years and shake their hands in fellowship? Wouldn't you like to exchange stories and jokes? Most of all, wouldn't you like to know how things worked out in life for them? Wouldn't it be an absolute honor to meet the teams of, say, 1917, 1929, 1932, 1941, 1945, 1950, 1957, any team in the sixties, or maybe even 2001?

If you could do this, would you say to them, "We shared the same Good Ground with you, and we had

Wayland Roberts, Jr., 1950.

our dreams, just as you had. Things never worked out the way we thought they might, but that's all right. All is well." Don't you suppose they would have the same curiosity about you and me?

May I share a personal thought with you? I'm pretty sure that the long line of black-and-gold uniformed players turned out just fine. I surmise this because I read the names of the players on each year's team and recognized many of them for the future leaders they became. I saw war heroes, coaches, schoolteachers, businessmen, politicians, athletes, and physicians. Among these young men, I saw Catholics, Protestants, and Jews, and eventually I saw young men of color.

Would it be a case of fantasy gone wild to imagine that late in the evening on a hot August night, with the only sound coming from the sprinklers trying to quench the thirst of the practice field, that shades emerge in their uniforms of varying vintage, take their seats on the side of the hill and engage in the good natured bantering that young men do so well?

Perhaps the tall and handsome Walter Terry of 1910 might challenge Paul Goad of 1951 to a foot race. Herbert Rule from 1920 could seize the opportunity to slap Sam Coots of 1942 on the back, happy to meet him. Off to one side Wayland Roberts from 1950 is arm wrestling Fred Williams from 1947 (careful Fred, Wayland is pretty strong)!

This is a joyous nightly reunion, no longer separated by the years—no, not by years or race or circumstance. Should the boys become too rowdy, which would not be surprising, Riley Johns will restore order. Coach Matthews will likely seek out his mentors, Earl Quigley and Raymond Burnett, for you see coaches have a place here too.

But wait! Another group approaches, not from the stadium, but from the school. Four generations of teachers have come by to say hello. Those wonderful teachers that spent their summers in graduate school to earn a master's degree, and who worked for us for years out of their love for their profession, and not just for a paycheck. There's my old Algebra teacher, Mr. W. P. Ivy, who always asks me if I believe in signs, referring not to the metaphysical but rather to my ineptness in algebraic addition. Miss Mary Craig is nearby too. She held a graduate degree from Columbia University, was an expert on Shakespeare, but more importantly, she made the arcane language of his plays come alive when she translated them for us.

Fifty years later, those teachers who remain, still come to our class reunions, often in wheel chairs, because even after all this time they still care, and they're still interested. These splendid men and women were as vital as anything to the Good Ground that we grew from.

And each night this congregation of souls watches to see if some new shade is trudging toward them from 14th Street. That happens frequently now. As daybreak approaches, they start to walk across the practice field back to the school or to the stadium, vanishing in the shadows. In a short time, the young men now in charge of Tiger history will regain custody of this Good Ground.

It is not necessary to burden a teenage boy with the heavy issues suggested above. It's quite enough for him to concentrate on blocking and tackling, but we can close with the judgment that the football field of Little Rock Central High School is symbolically Good Ground. If you wish, you can stoop down and run your fingers through the dirt and grass, but that's not the Good Ground. The Good Ground is the advantages the coaches, trainers, teachers, clergy, school board, and families tried to provide us to fulfill our potential as young men, and young women too. Indeed, this is very Good Ground.

CPSIA information can be obtained
at www.ICGtesting.com
Printed in the USA
FFOW01n0350030314
3946FF